BY DESIGN

Urban design in the planning system: towards better practice

COMMISSION FOR ARCHITECTURE
& THE BUILT ENVIRONMENT

After the General Election in June 2001 the responsibilities of the former Department of the Environment, Transport and the Regions (DETR) in this area were transferred to the new Department for Transport, Local Government and the Regions (DTLR).

Department for Transport, Local Government and the Regions
Eland House
Bressenden Place
London SW1E 5DU
Telephone: 020 7944 3000
Web site: www.dtlr.gov.uk

Commission for Architecture and the Built Environment
Tower Building, 11 York Road
London SE1 7NX
Telephone: 020 7960 2400
Fax: 020 7960 2444
Email: enquiries@cabe.org.uk

Design and Artwork by Tempo Graphic Design Limited

Further copies of this report are available from:

T¹ Thomas Telford *Publishing*

The Customer Services Department
Thomas Telford Ltd., Units I/K
Paddock Wood Distribution Centre
Paddock Wood, Tonbridge
Kent TN12 6UU
Tel: (020) 7665 2464
Fax: (020) 7665 2245

ISBN 0 7277 2937 3

Printed in Great Britain on material containing 75% post-consumer waste, 5% Pre-consumer waste and 20% TCF pulp by Latimer Trend & Company Limited.
May 2000
Reprinted 2001

CONTENTS

FOREWORD

Good urban design is essential if we are to produce attractive, high-quality, sustainable places in which people will want to live, work and relax. It is fundamental to our objective of an urban renaissance. We do not have to put up with shoddy, unimaginative and second-rate buildings and urban areas. There is a clamour for better designed places which inspire and can be cherished, places where vibrant communities can grow and prosper. To achieve this we need to effect a culture change, and this guide is designed to help this process.

It provides sound, practical advice to help implement the Government's commitment to good design, as set out in Planning Policy Guidance Note 1 General Policy and Principles. It encourages those who influence and shape development decisions to think more deeply and sensitively about the living environments being created. It reinforces the call in the Urban Task Force's report "Towards an Urban Renaissance" for earlier, greater and better-informed attention to urban design.

The guide has been drawn up around a limited number of simple but compelling principles. We want to draw out three in particular. First, good design is important everywhere, not least in helping to bring rundown, neglected places back to life. Second, while the planning system has a key role to play in delivering better design, the creation of successful places depends on the skills of designers and the vision and commitment of those who employ them. Finally, no two places are identical and there is no such thing as a blueprint for good design. Good design always arises from a thorough and caring understanding of place and context.

This Government showed its commitment to securing good urban design, when it created the Commission for Architecture and the Built Environment (CABE) last year, and gave them the task of taking the campaign for quality to the heart of Government and the outside world alike. CABE was therefore delighted to help in the production of this guide. We hope it will prompt both experts and relative newcomers to the field to think more deeply and carefully about the many complex issues that urban design is concerned with and to translate those thoughts into exciting and creative responses to design challenges. We believe that if it succeeds it will help to improve the quality of people's lives.

This is what good urban design is all about. A guide such as this cannot achieve it by itself. We hope that those who read it will be inspired by the message it contains and use its many suggestions to help them in the vitally important task of improving the quality of urban design throughout the country.

Nick Raynsford MP

Minister for Housing and
Planning

Stuart Lipton

Chairman
Commission for Architecture and the Built Environment

THE NEED FOR BETTER URBAN DESIGN

THE NEED FOR BETTER URBAN DESIGN

PURPOSE OF THE GUIDE

The aim of this guide is to promote higher standards in urban design. It does not set out new policy. The Government's policy for design in the planning system is contained in Planning Policy Guidance Note 1 *General Policy and Principles* (PPG1) and expounded further in other PPGs. The challenge in PPG1 is clear: "good design should be the aim of all those involved in the development process and should be encouraged everywhere".

This guide will help to encourage better design and is intended as a companion to the PPGs. But it is not intended to be the last word, nor should it be. It has been written to stimulate thinking about urban design, not to tell the reader how to design. The central message is that careful assessments of places, well-drafted policies, well-designed proposals, robust decision-making and a collaborative approach are needed throughout the country if better places are to be created.

The guide is relevant to all aspects of the built environment, including the design of buildings and spaces, landscapes and transport systems. It has implications for planning and development at every scale: in villages as well as cities and for a street and its neighbourhood as well as regional planning strategies.

Its main audience is expected to be officers and councillors in local authorities who guide and control development. But the guide will also be relevant to housebuilders and all those who promote new development and apply for planning permission. More widely, it will be of interest to anyone who wants to see greater care taken in the design of their neighbourhoods.

A striking fact is that many of the small developments that can cumulatively change a place dramatically are designed by people with little or no formal design training. Raising standards of urban design will depend in large part on whether the people behind these projects make more use of suitably qualified, skilled and experienced designers. It will also depend, as envisaged in PPG1, on high standards being set and upheld within the planning system.

URBAN DESIGN

Urban design is the art of making places for people. It includes the way places work and matters such as community safety, as well as how they look. It concerns the connections between people and places, movement and urban form, nature and the built fabric, and the processes for ensuring successful villages, towns and cities.

Urban design is a key to creating sustainable developments and the conditions for a flourishing economic life, for the prudent use of natural resources and for social progress. Good design can help create lively places with distinctive character; streets and public spaces that are safe, accessible, pleasant to use and human in scale; and places that inspire because of the imagination and sensitivity of their designers.

There are many benefits to be gained from thinking coherently about the way places are designed. Some are the traditional concerns of good planning, others are relatively new. For example, 'Secured by Design' promoted by the Association of Chief Police Officers has prompted greater attention to designing out crime and the fear of crime. More recently, the Urban Task Force led by Lord Rogers underlined the importance of good urban design to an urban renaissance. The Task Force's vision of towns and cities as places of opportunity and sustainable growth is largely founded on design excellence.

Urban design does not just concern one profession or interest group. This was underlined in 1998 when five professional institutes came together with other organisations and set up the Urban Design Alliance, finding a common purpose in working across their individual disciplines. These professions – town planners, landscape architects, surveyors, architects and civil engineers – can all be powerful influences for better urban design.

As the Urban Task Force pointed out, the best way to promote successful and sustainable regeneration, conservation and place-making is to think about urban design from the start of the planning and development process. Leaving urban design until the end can make the planning process slow, frustrating and a source of wasteful conflict, and is unlikely to lead to the best outcome in terms of quality.

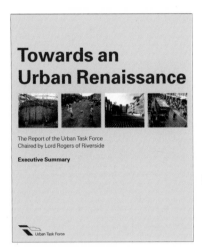

THE URBAN TASK FORCE, LED BY LORD ROGERS, EMPHASISED THE IMPORTANCE OF GOOD DESIGN

PLACE-MAKING

Successful urban design requires a full understanding of the conditions under which decisions are made and development is delivered. Many factors determine or influence the outcome of the design process and the sort of places we make. Success, nowadays, rarely happens by chance. It depends on:

- a clear framework provided by development plans and supplementary guidance delivered consistently, including through development control;

- a sensitive response to the local context;

- judgements of what is feasible in terms of economic and market conditions;

- an imaginative and appropriate design approach by those who design development and the people who manage the planning process.

It is vital to bring these factors together. If policy is not set out clearly for applicants, a proposed development may conflict unwittingly with a local authority's aspirations for good design. If too little weight is given to feasibility, the development may fail commercially. If too little weight is given to local context, the proposal may be opposed locally. If the design approach is wrong, the site's opportunities will be missed and poor or mediocre development will result.

THE ROLE OF THE PLANNING SYSTEM

The planning system provides the means to encourage good design, not just in conservation areas and other attractive places, but everywhere. Securing good design is central to good planning. The appearance of proposed development and its relationship to its surroundings are relevant to the consideration of a planning application and PPG1 makes it clear that local planning authorities should reject poor designs.

This guide looks at the 'tools' local authorities have available within the planning system to help deliver better design. The most important is the local authority's development plan. This should set out the design policies against which development proposals will be assessed. This guide considers both what could be included in the plan and how further explanation might be provided in supplementary guidance.

9

The development control process is vital. The way it is used determines whether and how the design policies in development plans and supplementary guidance are reflected and applied. The most thoroughly developed design policies will achieve little if they are ignored in the development control process. As stated in PPG1, "applicants for planning permission should be able to demonstrate how they have taken account of the need for good design in their development proposals and that they have had regard to relevant development plan policies and supplementary design guidance".

TOWARDS BETTER PRACTICE

Using the planning system effectively to create the conditions for better urban design requires positive management, meaningful collaboration and the right skills.

This guide offers suggestions to help create those conditions. It does not attempt to define a single blueprint for good urban design. Rather, as an aid to understanding, it seeks to describe some of the objectives of urban design. They relate to how people use buildings and urban space, and what they feel about the places they live and work in, and visit. The objectives are not unique to this guide and they could, and have been, described differently. What is attempted here is simply one description of what makes a successful place, based on widely shared experiences. Underlying it is the need to plan sustainable developments.

The objectives are supported by a series of considerations that can act as prompts to thinking about urban design. These prompts help to relate the objectives to the form of development – layout, scale, density, appearance and landscape. Achieving a successful relationship between objectives and development form depends on an intelligent response to local conditions.

An aim of this guide is to encourage a move away from a negative reliance on standards towards a more positive emphasis on performance criteria. Standards specify precisely how a development is to be designed (by setting out minimum distances between buildings, for example). Performance criteria are the means of assessing the extent to which a development fulfils a specific planning requirement (such as maintaining privacy). Imaginative designers can respond to performance criteria with a variety of design solutions.

Ultimately, achieving good design depends on the skills of the designer and the commitment to good design of all those concerned with new development. Better practice guidance cannot substitute for skilled designers and their ability to analyse places, to understand how they are used and experienced and to design with flair and sensitivity.

SECTION 2

THINKING ABOUT
URBAN DESIGN

THINKING ABOUT URBAN DESIGN

Good urban design is rarely brought about by a local authority prescribing physical solutions, or by setting rigid or empirical design standards but by approaches which emphasise design objectives or principles.

OBJECTIVES OF URBAN DESIGN

Successful streets, spaces, villages, towns and cities tend to have characteristics in common. These factors have been analysed to produce principles or objectives of good urban design. They help to remind us what should be sought to create a successful place. There is considerable overlap between the objectives and they are mutually re-inforcing.

14

OBJECTIVES OF URBAN DESIGN

CHARACTER
A place with its own identity

To promote character in townscape and landscape by responding to and reinforcing locally distinctive patterns of development, landscape and culture.

CONTINUITY AND ENCLOSURE
A place where public and private spaces are clearly distinguished

To promote the continuity of street frontages and the enclosure of space by development which clearly defines private and public areas.

QUALITY OF THE PUBLIC REALM
A place with attractive and successful outdoor areas

To promote public spaces and routes that are attractive, safe, uncluttered and work effectively for all in society, including disabled and elderly people.

EASE OF MOVEMENT
A place that is easy to get to and move through

To promote accessibility and local permeability by making places that connect with each other and are easy to move through, putting people before traffic and integrating land uses and transport.

LEGIBILITY
A place that has a clear image and is easy to understand

To promote legibility through development that provides recognisable routes, intersections and landmarks to help people find their way around.

ADAPTABILITY
A place that can change easily

To promote adaptability through development that can respond to changing social, technological and economic conditions.

DIVERSITY
A place with variety and choice

To promote diversity and choice through a mix of compatible developments and uses that work together to create viable places that respond to local needs.

ASPECTS OF DEVELOPMENT FORM

LAYOUT: URBAN STRUCTURE
The framework of routes and spaces that connect locally and more widely, and the way developments, routes and open spaces relate to one other.

The layout provides the basic plan on which all other aspects of the form and uses of a development depend.

LAYOUT: URBAN GRAIN
The pattern of the arrangement of street blocks, plots and their buildings in a settlement.

The degree to which an area's pattern of blocks and plot subdivisions is respectively small and frequent (fine grain), or large and infrequent (coarse grain).

LANDSCAPE
The character and appearance of land, including its shape, form, ecology, natural features, colours and elements, and the way these components combine.

This includes all open space, including its planting, boundaries and treatment.

DENSITY AND MIX
The amount of development on a given piece of land and the range of uses. Density influences the intensity of development, and in combination with the mix of uses can affect a place's vitality and viability.

The density of a development can be expressed in a number of ways. This could be in terms of plot ratio (particularly for commercial developments), number of dwellings, or the number of habitable rooms (for residential developments).

SCALE: HEIGHT
Scale is the size of a building in relation to its surroundings, or the size of parts of a building or its details, particularly in relation to the size of a person. Height determines the impact of development on views, vistas and skylines.

Height can be expressed in terms of the number of floors; height of parapet or ridge; overall height; any of these in combination; a ratio of building height to street or space width; height relative to particular landmarks or background buildings; or strategic views.

SCALE: MASSING
The combined effect of the arrangement, volume and shape of a building or group of buildings in relation to other buildings and spaces.

Massing is the three-dimensional expression of the amount of development on a given piece of land.

APPEARANCE: DETAILS
The craftsmanship, building techniques, decoration, styles and lighting of a building or structure.

This includes all building elements such as openings and bays; entrances and colonnades; balconies and roofscape; and the rhythm of the facade.

APPEARANCE: MATERIALS
The texture, colour, pattern and durability of materials, and how they are used.

The richness of a building lies in its use of materials which contribute to the attractiveness of its appearance and the character of an area.

16

ASPECTS OF DEVELOPMENT FORM

Urban design objectives are, by themselves, abstract. They have an impact on people's lives only by being translated into development. The form of buildings, structures and spaces is the physical expression of urban design. It is what influences the pattern of uses, activity and movement in a place, and the experiences of those who visit, live or work there. This guide sets out the most important characteristics of the physical form of development by articulating eight aspects. Together, these define the overall layout of the place (in terms of its routes and building blocks); its scale (in terms of building height and massing); its appearance (as expressed in details and use of materials); and its landscape (including all the public realm, built and green spaces).

OBJECTIVES AND DEVELOPMENT FORM BROUGHT TOGETHER

Effective design policy and design guidance is likely to focus on how, in a particular context, development form can achieve the urban design objectives.

The lists of objectives and aspects of form have been produced in order to encourage writers of policy and guidance and decision-makers to ask a series of questions that go deeper than generalisations. These questions should draw together urban design objectives and aspects of development form. For example, what form of layout would help to achieve a particular objective in this context? What scale? And so on, depending on what is considered relevant. Guidance based on such systematic thinking will help developers and designers by moving beyond simple exhortations that, for example, new development should be 'in character'.

Ultimately, the development form which emerges as a result of such a process is more likely to result in better designed places. Readers of this guide are encouraged to think in terms of objectives and form as they consider its advice and decide how to put it into practice in their own locality.

17

18

PROMPTS TO THINKING

The objectives are general and should be tailored to the locality. This process can be helped by the series of prompts to thinking about urban design set out in the next section of this guide. The prompts are unfolded under each of the urban design objectives but they are closely related and are not unique to the objective under which they appear.

Most importantly, they are prompts not rules. They are not rigid formulae to be followed slavishly.

In any real situation, some of these prompts will conflict and some will benefit some people more than others. Good design results from consideration being given to a wide range of concerns and the creative resolution of potential conflicts. For example, the height of a building might need to respond to a general pattern of buildings of no more than three storeys, to the potential of high density development for making the most of public transport and creating vitality, to the value of creating a landmark to enhance views, to the need for a sense of enclosure, to the opportunity to enhance safety by natural surveillance, and to the need to avoid overshadowing.

Each of these might indicate a different height for the building if they were to be considered separately. In the real world, the planning and design process must lead to a solution that takes all concerns into account. This depends on, first, a judgement of how important each is in the circumstances and, second, design skills capable of rising imaginatively to the demands of a difficult brief.

The prompts are followed by pointers to good design. Some prompts can be explained more simply than others, but this does not necessarily mean they are less important. Nor is the list exhaustive: evolving practice and special local conditions will always give rise to new ways of achieving better urban design.

RESPONDING TO LOCAL CHARACTER

A SUCCESSFUL PLACE BRINGS PEOPLE TOGETHER FOR DIFFERENT REASONS

The list of urban design objectives is used as the basis of the prompts which follow.

CHARACTER
A place with its own identity

The positive features of a place and its people contribute to its special character and sense of identity. They include landscape, building traditions and materials, patterns of local life, and other factors that make one place different from another. The best places are memorable, with a character which people can appreciate easily.

Many of the places which we now think of as being pleasantly distinctive grew naturally in response to local circumstances. Where such distinctiveness is ignored, new development may reflect only the marketing policies or corporate identities of national and international companies, the standard practices and products of the building industry, or the latest fashions among design professionals. Development that responds sensitively to the site and its setting, by contrast, is likely to create a place that is valued and pleasing to the eye.

Designing for local distinctiveness involves the creative reconciliation of local practices, on the one hand, with the latest technologies, building types and needs, on the other. Where there are no significant local traditions, the challenge to create a distinctive place will be all the greater. There is no reason why character and innovation should not go together. New and old buildings can coexist happily without disguising one as the other, if the design of the new is a response to urban design objectives.

LANDSCAPE IS AN IMPORTANT PART OF LOCAL IDENTITY

Consider the site's land form and character when laying out new development.

— The three-dimensional shape of the landscape is the basis for a development's form (expressed in its layout and massing). Natural features can help give shape to a development and integrate it into the wider area, contributing to a sense of place.

— Conserving a site's natural features provides for a better relationship between new development and its environment. Natural features include rivers and streams, wetlands, ponds and lakes, hills, trees, wildlife habitats and rock outcrops.

— The local ecology can help to determine the character and identity of both a development and the place of which it is a part.

 THE MODERN BUILDING ON THE RIGHT RESPONDS TO THE ROBUST CHARACTER OF TRADITIONAL DEVELOPMENT IN LONDON DOCKLANDS

19

20

Integrating new development into its landscape setting reduces its impact on nature and reinforces local distinctiveness.

– The layout, massing and landscape design of development can be integrated successfully into the wider landscape through using structure planting, shelter belts, green wedges, and (along natural features, roads, rivers and canals) green corridors.

– Reflecting plant species that are common locally will help planting in new development to reinforce the distinct natural qualities of a place.

– Integrating new and existing development at their boundaries maintains the continuity of urban form and landscape.

SKYLINES ARE SENSITIVE TO BEING OBSCURED BY HIGH BUILDINGS IN FRONT OF EXISTING BUILDINGS OR HAVING THEIR SILHOUETTE SPOILED BY HIGH BUILDINGS BEHIND THEM

Responding to the existing layout of buildings, streets and spaces ensures that adjacent buildings relate to one another, streets are connected and spaces complement one another.

– The existing layout of an area reflects its history, functions and connections with adjoining areas. These can contribute to the interest and richness of new development, and to its potential to accommodate further change in future.

– Integrating existing buildings and structures into new development can maintain the continuity of the built fabric as well as retaining buildings of local distinctiveness, historic or townscape merit.

– Narrow plot widths promote more active frontages, increase the sense of enclosure and allow higher densities. They are particularly appropriate where they reflect existing settlement patterns.

Responding to local building forms and patterns of development in the detailed layout and design of development helps to reinforce a sense of place.

– Local building forms and details contribute to the distinctive qualities of a place. These can be successfully interpreted in new development without necessarily restricting the scope of the designer. Standard solutions are rarely acceptable, as they are unlikely to create a distinctive identity or make good use of a particular site.

– Local building forms sometimes include distinct housing types, boundary treatments, building lines, roof slopes, window types and gardens.

– Responding to such forms and practices should only be at the appropriate scale. The common practice of inflating traditional domestic forms to larger scales is generally to be avoided.

The use of local materials, building methods and details is a major factor in enhancing local distinctiveness.

— The scale, texture and colour of building materials reflects an area's special function and character.

— Every element of the street scene contributes to the identity of the place, including sculpture, lighting, railings, litter bins, paving, fountains and street furniture.

— Development can be enhanced by reflecting local art and craft traditions. These might relate to elements such as ironwork, stained glass, thatching, brickwork, masonry, walling and paving. They should not be add-ons or after-thoughts, but part of the design from the start.

The scale, massing and height of proposed development should be considered in relation to that of adjoining buildings; the topography; the general pattern of heights in the area; and views, vistas and landmarks.

— Relating new development to the general pattern of building heights should not preclude a degree of variety to reflect particular circumstances. The character of townscape depends on how individual buildings contribute to a harmonious whole, through relating to the scale of their neighbours and creating a continuous urban form.

— On a sloping site, buildings that sit on the real ground and step up the hill are more likely to contribute to local character and avoid blank walls at ground level than large monolithic slabs that ignore the topography.

— The massing of development contributes to creating distinctive skylines in cities, towns and villages, or to respecting existing skylines. The character of a skyline is composed of the massing of blocks and the shape of roofs, as well as by the height of buildings. A building

should only stand out from the background of buildings if it contributes positively to views and vistas as a landmark. Buildings which have functions of civic importance are one example.

CREATING A CLEARLY DEFINED URBAN EDGE

CONTINUITY AND ENCLOSURE
A place where public and private spaces are clearly distinguished

Development either contributes to making the urban fabric coherent or undermines it. Urban design is often a matter of adopting good manners, recognising that every building is part of a greater whole. Too many places have been blighted by development which, even if its design has merits seen in isolation, ignores its local urban structure and creates bits of leftover space that contribute nothing to the living village, town or city.

Successful urban space (including street space) is defined and enclosed by buildings, structures and landscape. The relationship between buildings on a street, and between buildings and the street, are the key to this. Buildings which follow a continuous building line around a street block and contain the private space within back yards or courtyards are often more successful than individual buildings that stand in the middle of a site. Buildings with live edges, such as shopfronts, doors directly to the street, or residential upper floors, enable people to keep an eye on public space and make it feel safer.

21

Buildings that relate to a common building line reinforce and define the street.

— Development that follows the boundary of the street block can help to create an unambiguous distinction between public and private spaces. Respecting the historic or traditional building line helps to integrate new development into the street scene, maintains the continuous urban fabric and avoids places of concealment.

— Continuous street frontages have a minimum of blank walls and gaps between buildings. Gaps between buildings reduce the degree to which the street is overlooked, as do blank walls (which also encourage graffiti). There are places, however, such as some villages where strong building lines are not a dominant feature of the street scene.

— Projections and setbacks from the building line, such as bays and entrances add valuable emphasis without undermining the principle of continuity.

— Where buildings step back from the common building line, they can create usable, attractive spaces for pedestrians.

— Small setbacks can be used to soften the impact that buildings and the public realm have on each other.

The primary access to a building is best achieved from the street.

— Building entrances that are clearly identifiable contribute to the ease of understanding a place. Entrances are where people move between public and private space and create activity on the street.

— Direct access to the street from ground floor premises (both housing and shops), rather than by way of communal entrances, can reduce the length of blank facades.

— Primary access to buildings by means of internal courtyards reduces street activity and the live connection between building and street.

— Access to private or communal back yards, such as for parking, requires careful control by means of gates or by overlooking.

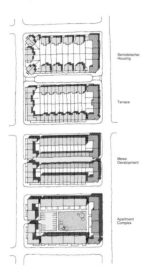

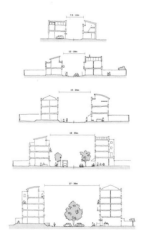

PERIMETER BLOCKS CAN WORK AT ANY SCALE

THE SCALE OF BUILDINGS SHOULD RELATE TO THE WIDTH OF THE STREET

The front and backs of buildings are often used in different ways, their design can reflect this.

— Designing the less private rooms (such as living rooms) to face the street, particularly at the ground floor, means the front of a building can have a direct relationship with the street.

— More private rooms such as bedrooms and bathrooms contribute little or nothing to overlooking the street and tend to deaden the street frontage.

— Buildings which present their backs to public space (even on main roads) often present high fences and walls to the street, reducing overlooking and safety. A separate boulevard-type slip road is a way of enabling buildings to front onto main roads where access is restricted.

Clearly defining and enclosing private space at the back of buildings provides for better privacy and security.

— Back yards or inner courtyards that are private or communally shared space are best enclosed by the backs of buildings.

— The rear gardens of houses are more secure if they back on to other gardens, rather than side roads, service lanes or footpaths.

— Where shared (but not public) space is provided in internal courtyards of high density housing developments, the privacy of ground floor rear rooms can be protected by private yards or gardens. These need to be clearly defined by walls or other boundary treatments.

Development can help define streets and public spaces.

— Streets, squares, parks and other spaces can be defined by appropriately scaled buildings and trees. The height of buildings should relate to the width and importance of the space

(including streets) which they enclose. The massing and height of a building should also have regard to the degree to which it will overlook and overshadow other buildings.

— A building at the corner of a street block can turn and close the corner visually. Shallower building depths can be used at the corners of street blocks, to allow sunlight and daylight to penetrate without interrupting the continuous building line round the block's perimeter. Relaxing standards (for minimum garden sizes and back-to-gable distances) can reduce or even eliminate gaps and blank walls when housing turns the corner. This also increases privacy to the rear.

— Setbacks at upper floors reduce a building's impact at street level by allowing one or more upper storeys to be less visible from the street. Setting back can allow an increase in density without an equivalent increase in the sense of scale but when overdone it can result in over-development and block light.

Defining the relationship between the fronts of buildings and the street benefits their respective uses.

— Clearly indicating the extent of private ownership of space round a building (by means such as walls, fences, railings, gates, arches, signage and paving) defines the boundary between public and private space.

— Detailed design can make clear whether ambiguous spaces (such as forecourts, malls, arcades and covered streets) are public or private.

BUILDINGS AT POUNDBURY OPEN DIRECTLY ONTO THE STREET IN THE TRADITIONAL WAY

23

QUALITY OF THE PUBLIC REALM
a place with attractive and successful outdoor areas

The success of the public realm depends on the arrangement of its paving, planting, lighting, orientation, shelter, signage, street furniture, and the way it is overlooked, as well as the routes which pass through it, and the uses in and next to it.

The public realm is made up of the parts of a village, town or city that are available, without special charge, for use by everyone. This can include streets, parks, squares, arcades and public buildings, whether publicly or privately owned. It provides the setting not only for everyday life, but also for more formal civic occasions. It is enlarged and enriched by developments designed to welcome a broad range of people, and by creative management. It is restricted and impoverished by buildings and spaces designed to keep out or discourage all but a narrow range of users, and by over-regulation. Anyone who is designing a building, or any other structure, is helping to shape the public realm.

How attractive a public space is, and how well people treat it, will partly depend on the arrangements made for its management and on how easy it is to maintain.

A successful place has a system of open and green spaces that respect natural features and are accessible.

– Public spaces can be designed to create a variety of type of space (path, street, square, park, plaza, green), character of space (informal, civic, recreational, commercial) and scale of space, rather than being merely the parts of an area that have not been built on. The provision of public spaces should respond to the needs established by the patterns of local economic, social and cultural life.

– Well-designed public spaces are functioning parts of a network of pedestrian routes, providing for the needs of all users including disabled and elderly people.

– Streets and street junctions that are designed as public spaces (rather than just traffic routes) are likely to be more convenient for all users.

– Street trees and street lighting can reinforce the character and relative importance of a route.

– Making use of natural assets such as water, riversides, slopes, trees and other planting helps to create attractive spaces and encourages biodiversity.

Ground floors occupied by uses that relate directly to passing pedestrians create activity and interest.

– Facades can be enlivened by active uses (such as shops and restaurants), entrances, colonnades, and windows (views into the building give interest to passers-by and make the building's function apparent, while views out of the building facilitate overlooking, which contributes to safety).

– Privacy for ground floors of residential development on busy streets can be maintained by raising the floor above street level.

– Street entrances at frequent intervals help to ensure activity.

VICTORIA SQUARE, BIRMINGHAM: SUCCESSFULLY REMADE AS
A CIVIC AND PEDESTRIAN FOCUS

— Buildings on busy street corners that are designed to accommodate shops, restaurants and other similar activities can contribute to local identity and activity.

Well-designed public space relates to the buildings around it.

— Public space should be designed with a purpose in mind. Space left over after development, without a function, is a wasted resource and will detract from a place's sense of identity. It is likely to be abused and vandalised, diminishing safety and security.

Streets and spaces that are overlooked allow natural surveillance, feel safer and generally are safer.

— Buildings of all types which front on to streets, squares or parks, contribute to overlooking by showing their public face.

— Making separate footpaths or cycle tracks as direct as possible, and well overlooked, will help avoid producing places where pedestrians and cyclists feel unsafe.

— There are advantages in play areas, other communal space and parked cars being overlooked.

— Living over shops encourages natural supervision and evening activity.

— Lighting and planting can help or hinder surveillance and perceptions of safety.

The design of public spaces should take account of the micro-climate.

— The layout and massing of development should take account of local climatic conditions, including daylight and sunlight, wind, temperature and frost pockets.

— The micro-climate will both influence and be influenced by the form of development, including the orientation of buildings and the degree of enclosure.

— Public spaces should be protected from down-draughts from tall buildings, as well as from lateral winds.

— Deciduous trees and climbers can filter heat and pollution in summer and allow low winter sunlight.

MEETING ACCESSIBILITY STANDARDS CAN INSPIRE CREATIVE SOLUTIONS

HIGH QUALITY MATERIALS FOR SHARED SPACES

25

Works of art and well-designed street furniture integrated into the design of public spaces give identity and enhance the sense of place.

- Co-ordinating the design of streetscape avoids clutter and confusion. This includes all elements of the street scene including signage, lighting, railings, litter bins, paving, seating, bus shelters, bollards, kiosks, cycle racks as well as sculpture and fountains.

- Streetscape design should take account of the need for maintenance, resistance to vandalism and access to underground services.

- The work of artists should be integrated into the design process at the earliest possible stage if it is to be used effectively.

- Street furniture such as benches and bus stops should be sited with the safety of users in mind.

EVERY ITEM OF STREET FURNITURE ◮
IS A POTENTIAL WORK OF ART

THE EXPERIENCE OF THE PUBLIC ◮
REALM IS ENRICHED BY DETAILS

EASE OF MOVEMENT
A place that is easy to get to and move through

The convenience, safety and comfort with which people go to and pass through buildings, places and spaces play a large part in determining how successful a place will be. Streets are more than just traffic channels for vehicles, and should offer a safe and attractive environment for all. Well-designed streets encourage people to use them, and make going outside a safe and pleasant experience.

Successful places are unlikely to include large blocks of inward-looking development which exclude public access.

A well-designed urban structure has a network of connected spaces and routes, for pedestrians, cyclists and vehicles.

- New routes should connect into existing routes and movement patterns. The degree of connection in a new development is often the key to its success. Established footpaths, shortcuts and minor roads can become the basis of enduring linkages.

- Public transport should be designed as an integral part of the street layout.

- Minimising walking distances between major land uses and public transport stops makes public transport easier to use and available to as many people as possible.

- A junction can be designed as a point of entry. Such junctions can help identify a place and define the routes through.

Transport routes should reflect urban design qualities and not just traffic considerations.

- Streets should be designed as public spaces not just in response to engineering considerations.

– Boulevards are a means of creating continuous frontage development and providing a high level of traffic capacity.

– The traditional form of high street, which allows for stopping, parking and slow traffic, provides an effective way of accommodating local shopping and economic activity.

A development's access and circulation should contribute to a fine-grain network of direct and connected routes within and beyond the site rather than creating big blocks.

– The grain of streets is usually finer around busy shopping streets.

– Streets that connect to other streets encourage movement and activity and short linked-up streets can make places more accessible and encourage walking and cycling.

– In designing for connected streets care should be taken to avoid undermining the 'defensible space' of particular neighbourhoods.

The way development is laid out can encourage low traffic speeds.

– Developments should be designed with regard to their effect on traffic speeds.

– Traffic speeds can be managed by the arrangement of buildings and spaces. Physical traffic-calming measures should be secondary but considered as an integral part of the design.

– Changes in materials or 'gateways' at the entrance to low speed areas can alert motorists to the need to reduce speed.

– Smaller corner radii will encourage more careful vehicle movement.

The layout and density of development can help increase accessibility to public transport.

– Higher densities help to support public transport.

Integrated transport interchanges promote the use of public transport and provide for seamless movement between all modes of travel.

– Higher density commercial and mixed-use developments, civic buildings and developments likely to generate large numbers of visitors are best located within close walking distance of public transport interchanges.

– Stations designed as an integral part of the public realm create safe and secure pedestrian environments at all times of the day.

PUBLIC TRANSPORT AS AN INTEGRAL PART OF THE STREET

THE NEW CENTRAL SQUARE AT BIRMINGHAM'S BRINDLEYPLACE LINKS TO THE CITY CENTRE'S MAIN PEDESTRIAN ROUTE

LEGIBILITY
A place that has a clear image and is easy to understand

Landmarks, gateways and focal points help people find their way. Vistas create visual links between places. Planting can emphasise pedestrian routes. Visible routes and destinations, and a visible choice of routes, will contribute to making a place feel safe and unthreatening. Places where form, layout and signage make them easy to understand are likely both to function well and to be pleasant to live in or visit.

Equally, some places draw their charm from their lack of clear routes. The process of design needs to take account of the fact that people do not all read, interpret and enjoy a place in the same way. Men and women, children and adults, residents and visitors, old and young people, and people from different cultures will experience it differently and be encouraged to feel at ease by different aspects.

Development that is sited so as to enhance existing views and vistas, and create new ones, can help people to find their way around.

– The ability to see important routes and landmarks can be integral to finding one's way around and in reinforcing the sense of place.

– Where possible, views should focus on important routes, memorable buildings and landscape features.

– A sense of place often depends on the design of the public realm and its contribution to an area's character and identity. Bespoke design can help, not least of street furniture.

A DIRECTION AID DOES NOT HAVE TO BE SOMETHING TO READ

The design, location and function of buildings can reinforce the identity and character of the routes and spaces they serve.

– Concentrating the most active uses on main routes and around focal points will contribute to the vitality of a place.

– Civic and community buildings, located around public spaces, provide symbols of community identity and a focus for civic life.

LOCAL IDENTITY IS A KEY TO LEGIBILITY

SOMETHING
MEMORABLE
IS WORTH
A HUNDRED
SIGNS

— The choice of materials can add interest and aid legibility. The infinite variations in any natural material have their own intrinsic qualities and uniqueness.

— The quality of signage, including that for shops and other commercial premises, is important and can enhance identity and legibility.

— Works of art and lighting schemes can help to aid identity and legibility.

— Ensuring that a public building's function is readily apparent to passers-by and that its main entrance is easily identifiable contributes to the ease of understanding a place.

Well-designed corners enhance legibility by creating visual interest and contributing to a distinctive identity.

— Corner buildings can provide identity and points of orientation. Making them higher than the surrounding buildings will emphasise their importance.

— Locating public uses such as shops on the corners of busy streets enhances activity and local identity.

The legibility of an area can be improved through the detailing and quality of materials in new development.

— Legible designs often depend on close attention being paid to the detailing, for example of shopfronts and building entrances.

— Richness of detail is particularly important at ground level, where people see it close at hand.

ADAPTABILITY
A place that can change easily

The most successful places have prospered in changing circumstances. Even though people may live, travel and work in very different ways, the basic structure of the physical fabric of such places proves to be grounded in unchanging patterns of human life, rather than being unalterably fitted to some very specific purpose. Successful places avoid the destructive trauma of large-scale blight and dereliction, and the sort of comprehensive redevelopment which serves a narrowly-defined range of purposes.

Places need to be adaptable at every scale. A household makes different demands on a house as children are born and grow up. Towns and cities as a whole have to adapt as industries rise and decline, demand for housing and the nature of workplaces changes, and buildings and infrastructure age.

DISTINCTIVE BUILDINGS HELP PEOPLE FIND THEIR WAY AROUND

29

Simple, robust building forms, not tightly designed to a very particular use allow for the greatest variety of possible future uses to be accommodated.

–   Floor-to-ceiling heights and building depths should be considered in the light of the need for flexibility to allow later conversion of a building to other uses.

–   Adaptable ground floors on corners of busy streets allow different uses to be accommodated over time.

–   Well-designed housing is adaptable to the changing needs of its occupants.

THE UNDIVIDED GROUND FLOOR SPACES IN MEWS BUILDINGS MAKE THEM EASY TO ADAPT. SUCH FLEXIBILITY CAN BE DESIGNED INTO NEW BUILDINGS

A DUTCH BARN CONVERTED INTO OFFICES AND STABLES

Places should be capable of being used for a range of activities.

–   Well-designed public spaces allow for different uses, such as events, festivals and markets.

–   Development can be related to the public realm in ways that encourage rather than discourage flexible use of buildings and space. This can be achieved through the imaginative use of elements such as terraces, balconies and forecourts.

–   To encourage a mix of uses buildings can be designed so as to facilitate different access arrangements at different times.

Developments that endure have flexible layouts and design.

–   Fine-grain development is easier to adapt than large-scale megastructures.

–   Roads within a development which are built to adoptable standards, rather than being locked into estate management agreements (which inhibit change), will allow a greater variety of uses to be developed over time.

–   The layout of the infrastructure servicing development (including water supply, sewerage, drainage, gas, electricity, cable, telephone, roads, footpaths, cycleways and parks) should take account of foreseeable changes in demand.

–   Building to last means thinking about future uses, expansion and changing needs for access. For example, the location of means of escape can facilitate a building's later conversion, the position of the building on its site can affect scope for expansion, and floor-to-ceiling heights are important in this context.

LOFT CONVERSIONS TAKE ADVANTAGE OF ⬥
ROBUST BUILDING FORMS

LONG-LIFE, LOOSE-FIT STRUCTURES ⬥
HAVE FLEXIBILITY BUILT IN

THE ADAPTABLE FORM OF THIS FORMER ⬥
COMMERCIAL BUILDING ALLOWED IT TO BE
CONVERTED TO HOUSING WHEN THE
MARKET CHANGED.

DIVERSITY
A place with variety and choice

The mix of uses (whether within a building, a street or an area) can help to determine how well-used a place is, and what economic and social activities it will support.

A mix of uses may be appropriate at a variety of scales: within a village, town or city; within a neighbourhood or a street; or even in a particular building. In a town centre, for example, housing can provide customers for shops, make use of empty space above them and generate activity when they are closed. In residential areas, workplaces, shops and other facilities can make the place more than just a dormitory.

Mixed-use development can make the most of opportunities for higher densities and intensive activity at locations with good access to public transport. At higher densities, it can provide the sort of environment that will suit particular kinds of household, such as single or young people, or couples without children.

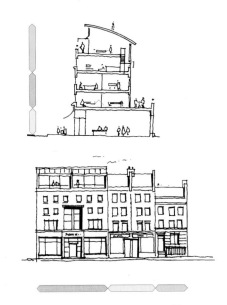

MIXED USES WITHIN A BUILDING ⬥
(TOP) AND ON A STREET

31

Creating a mix of uses can help to attract people to live, work and play in the same area.

– The mix can be at the scale of the building (one use above another), the street (one use next to another) or the neighbourhood (groups of uses next to others).

– Vital places often have a mix of uses which involves different people using the same parts of a building or place at different times of the day, as well as different uses happening in different parts of a building or space at the same time.

Getting the mix right is important.

– A successful mix of uses results where the uses are compatible one with another and interact with each other positively.

– A successful mix of uses is achieved where the uses help to create a balanced community with a range of services, without increasing reliance on the car.

OXO TOWER WHARF ON LONDON'S SOUTH BANK MIXES DIFFERENT USES ON DIFFERENT FLOORS

Diversity of layout, building form and tenure can contribute to making successful living and working environments.

– Buildings of different sizes and types allow for different uses to be accommodated over time.

– To promote social inclusion, in well-designed places social housing is not distinguishable from private housing by its design, nor is it banished to the least attractive site.

– Subdividing large sites into smaller development plots, each with direct access to public roads or spaces, can help create diversity, especially if different approaches to design are adopted, using different architects.

– Narrow plot frontages can allow small-scale shopping and commercial activities to flourish and adapt to changing needs.

BIRMINGHAM'S BRINDLEYPLACE IS A MAJOR COMMERCIAL MIXED-USE DEVELOPMENT

URBAN DESIGN AND THE PLANNING TOOLKIT

UNDERSTANDING THE LOCAL CONTEXT

THE DEVELOPMENT PLAN

SUPPLEMENTARY PLANNING GUIDANCE

DEVELOPMENT CONTROL

URBAN DESIGN AND THE PLANNING TOOLKIT

A better practice guide can only hope to convey a general appreciation of why urban design matters. It can offer prompts for better design but successful development depends on tailoring these to local circumstances in both drawing up and implementing planning policies. Development plan policies and supplementary planning guidance should be drawn up so as to reflect local needs and opportunities. Design policies cannot take a standard format or be imported from another area. Everything hangs on how well a local authority draws up, and then uses, the tools it has available to foster better urban design.

UNDERSTANDING THE LOCAL CONTEXT

Understanding the local context should be the prelude to drawing up the planning 'toolkit'. Developing this understanding will involve considering a wide range of matters. Some will be matters of simple observation or professional judgement. Others will be matters of opinion, raising questions about whose perspective counts in the particular circumstances, and how those people are to be involved in the process of appraising the context. A range of techniques is available, but carrying out an appraisal is more important than the specific technique used and a simple assessment is better than none.

An appraisal can consist of three elements; the emphasis will differ depending, for example, on whether the aim is to produce policy for a plan or a brief for a specific site. First, there is likely to be a mainly qualitative assessment of how the area performs in terms of urban design objectives. Second, the characteristics of the area or site could be assessed in terms of constraints, opportunities and capacity for development. Finally, those factors which overlay the local context, such as government advice, would need to be built into the appraisal.

ANALYSING PERFORMANCE IN TERMS OF URBAN DESIGN

The urban design objectives set out earlier can be used to order the considerations relevant to appraisal. What follows is, in effect, a series of checklists. They are not meant to be followed slavishly. Understanding the local context does not require every item on the checklists to be examined on every occassion and in every place or in the same depth. The checklists provide pointers to understanding an area in terms of its urban design.

CHARACTER
A place with its own identity

A variety of techniques is available for appraising the unique qualities of a place and its people. These include observation and site surveys, reviewing historic records, interviews with local amenity groups, and wider public consultation.

Appraisals can include assessments of:
- memories and associations, local traditions and cultural diversity;
- the origins and development of the topography of the area, including surviving elements of historic street patterns, plot subdivisions,

boundary treatments and the relationships between buildings and spaces;

- the archaeological significance and potential of the area;
- the architecture and historic quality, character and coherence of buildings, both listed and unlisted, and the contribution they make to the special interest of the area;
- the character and hierarchy of spaces and their townscape quality;
- prevalent and historic building materials;
- the contribution made to the character of the area by green spaces, trees, hedges and other cultivated elements;
- the area's prevailing (or former) uses, plan forms and building types;
- the relationship of the built environment to landscape or open countryside, including significant landmarks, vistas and panoramas;
- features which have been lost, or which intrude on or detract from the character of the area.

- active and dead frontages at ground floor level: positive factors such as entrances, shopfronts and windows; and negative factors such as long blank facades and high boundary walls, solid roller shutters to shopfronts, and service entrances and yards;
- active and dead frontages at upper floors: positive factors such as windows of habitable rooms overlooking public space; and negative factors such as blank gable walls and unused space over shops;
- places where buildings meet the public realm: boundary treatments such as changes of level; gates, railings, fences and boundary walls; front gardens and in-curtilage parking; and servicing;
- spatial enclosure: cross-sectional studies examine the relationship between the heights of buildings and the spaces they define;
- planting (such as trees and hedges), natural features, land form, and retaining walls which define and enclose blocks and spaces.

CONTINUITY AND ENCLOSURE
A place where public and private spaces are clearly distinguished

The appraisal of the continuity of building frontages and the degree of enclosure of blocks and public spaces is largely based on site surveys, and studies of the dimensions of buildings and streets.

Techniques include identifying and mapping:
- gap sites and abnormal setbacks which interrupt the common building line of the street;
- conflicts between the backs and fronts of buildings and the fronts of others, and instances where the backs of buildings are exposed to public view and access (as in the case of back gardens on to roads, alleys and public spaces);

QUALITY OF THE PUBLIC REALM
A place with attractive and successful outdoor areas

Appraisals of the public realm are based largely on looking at its components in terms of condition, fitness for purpose, and contribution to local and civic identity, and at the potential for reducing street clutter.

Traffic Measures in Historic Towns (Civic Trust and English Historic Towns Forum, 1993) provides a valuable checklist for assessing how street clutter can be reduced. Appraisals can be supplemented by detailed mapping using Geographical Information System (GIS) techniques and surveys of users, and by looking at local crime and accident statistics.

Public realm audits can include assessments of:
- hard landscaping (paving materials, kerbs, walls, steps and ramps);

- planting (trees, planters, grassed areas, flowers and borders);
- street furniture (seats, bins, bollards, manhole covers, tree grilles and railings);
- structures (bus shelters, kiosks, stalls, information points, pedestrian bridges, beacons and temporary structures);
- banners and signs (interpretative, instructive, informative, and directional);
- lighting (pavement, pedestrian, highway, security, building and feature);
- public art and features (permanent and temporary works, fountains and graphics);
- shopfronts (thresholds, glazing, stall risers, signs, banners and shutters).
- advertisements (hoardings, kiosks and banners);
- special treatments and provision (use of colour, tactile paving, wheelchair ramps, dock edge treatments);
- safety and security (emergency equipment, salt and grit bins, closed-circuit television, gates and grilles);
- traffic and highways installations (including highway markings, parking meters, traffic signals and control boxes);
- public space use and management (informal use as well as formal, events, markets, graffiti removal, litter collection and street cleansing).

EASE OF MOVEMENT
A place that is easy to get to and move through

All types of movement in an area can be appraised, in terms of strategic and local accessibility, traffic passing and arriving, and the potential for shifting the balance from cars to walking, cycling and public transport. Such appraisals will largely rely on survey information and statistical analysis of already available data. Existing information held in local authorities, by passenger transport operators, town centre management and retail research organisations (for pedestrian flows in town centres) and local businesses can be supplemented by additional surveys and counts.

PPG 13 *Transport: a guide to better practice* provides a checklist for an audit of transport conditions in an area.

Assessing ease of movement includes the following subjects:

- catchment areas;
- public transport services and accessibility, including modal split, trip patterns and journey times, interchange characteristics, levels of service and priority measures;
- cycle use, including routes and facilities;
- car use (and car ownership levels) including access and circulation and traffic flows;
- parking (on- and off-street);
- accessibility for disabled people, including gradients and obstructions;
- pedestrian movements including pedestrian counts (at various times of the day and week), points of arrival and destinations, pedestrian crossings and barriers to movement, points of conflict with other road users and overcrowding and congestion. Fruin analysis can be used to assess levels of comfort on pedestrian routes.
- connections through the area (these can be assessed by examining network characteristics, sightlines and the relationship of access to land use. Space syntax analysis is one technique that can help in this).

△ SPACE SYNTAX IS A TECHNIQUE FOR MEASURING HOW WELL STREETS ARE CONNECTED

LEGIBILITY
A place that has a clear image and is easy to understand

How easy a place is to understand can be assessed through a variety of techniques, including mapping, carrying out surveys and interviews, and watching how people behave.

Kevin Lynch developed techniques for analysing the local context which include appraisals of:
- gateways and points of transition (at main entry points, between different areas and at transitions between different uses);
- nodes (important junctions and points of interaction);
- landmarks and features (important buildings, corners, symbols and works of public art);
- views and vistas (seen from within the area and from the outside);
- edges, seams and barriers (including the boundaries between different zones and areas, and streets which integrate or sever).

ADAPTABILITY
A place that can change easily

Adaptability can be appraised through surveys of buildings and spaces, and by looking at how they are used. The level of detail will depend on the circumstances.

Buildings can be assessed in terms of:
- occupancy and tenure;
- building type (such as warehouse, commercial office block, terraced house);
- plan form, including building floorplate dimensions (window-to-window and floor-to-ceiling);
- access and circulation, including alternative means of escape, servicing and vertical circulation;

- adjacent buildings' uses;
- structural condition;
- service areas and access cores;
- suitability for modernisation or conversion to other uses.

Spaces can be assessed in terms of:
- ownership and tenure;
- access and circulation;
- overshadowing and micro-climate;
- surrounding buildings and their uses;
- layout including planting, paving, lighting and street furniture;
- shape, scale and slope.

DIVERSITY
A place with variety and choice

The degree of diversity a place offers can be assessed by looking at how buildings and spaces are used, and at patterns of ownership and occupancy.

Surveys will show:
- broad patterns of land use (precincts and quarters);
- patterns of sub-divisions of blocks (typical frontage dimensions and depth of block);
- distribution and amounts of land uses (residential, commercial, retail, community and employment) at street level and upper floors;
- social mix (private and social housing);
- ownership and tenure.

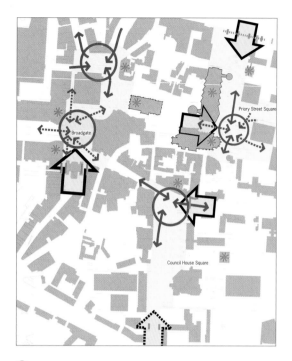

LYNCHIAN ANALYSIS FOCUSES ON THE FEATURES WHICH MAKE A PLACE EASY TO UNDERSTAND

40

IDENTIFYING CONSTRAINTS AND OPPORTUNITIES

An analysis of constraints and opportunities draws on the assessment of how the site or area is performing. It is not independent of the policy context. This mainly quantitative process can establish the capacity for growth or change.

Assessments will include:

- planning context (current policies, applications and consents);

- strategic context (links to the wider area and relationships to surrounding development);

- local and immediate context (adjacent land uses and links to the area or site);

- site and statistics (size, proportions, boundary definition);

- site and area characteristics (contours, ecology, landscape, hydrology, ground conditions, crime pattern analysis);

- site and area infrastructure (roads, services, utilities);

- statutory constraints (listed buildings, tree preservation orders);

- development feasibility, including an assessment of market demand;

- important structuring elements such as axes, historic routes, watersheds and main points of site access;

- tissue studies, which use tracing or overprinting to show comparisons between existing patterns of development on a site or area and well-known developments in other places; such studies can help to show a site's or area's capacity for development and suggest how it may be laid out.

THE GRAIN OF BLOCKS AND PLOTS CAN PROVIDE CLUES ABOUT HOW TO INTEGRATE DEVELOPMENT INTO ITS SETTING

TISSUE STUDIES CAN HELP IN DETERMINING THE CAPACITY OF A SITE OR AREA

INFLUENCES ON THE LOCAL POLICY CONTEXT

Local authorities operate the planning system within a framework of policy set by central government. The planning system itself is only one of the many influences on the design of buildings and spaces. Making the most of the potential for good design depends on understanding these influences and responding to them effectively.

In particular, national planning policy guidance, mostly in the form of Planning Policy Guidance Notes (PPGs), issued by the Department of the Environment, Transport and the Regions, needs to be taken into account. The issue of design is covered primarily in PPG1, though most PPGs provide some guidance on design:

PPG1 *General Policy and Principles* – sets out guidance on the role of design considerations in planning, emphasising that good design is a key aim;

PPG3 *Housing* – calls for high quality design, landscaping and open space in housing development and stresses the value of development briefs in raising design standards;

PPG6 *Town Centres and Retail Development* – promotes town centre strategies based on urban design analysis, providing a policy framework and the context for development briefs. It calls for improved standards of design of street furniture, paving, signage and car parks;

PPG7 *The Countryside: environmental quality and economic and social development* – promotes high standards of design and points to the role of Countryside Design Summaries, Village Design Statements and landscape character assessments;

PPG13, *Transport* – requires new development to help create places that connect with each other sustainably; the aim is to provide the right conditions to encourage walking, cycling and the use of public transport and to put people before traffic;

PPG15, *Conservation Areas and Listed Buildings* – encourages detailed control of the external appearance of buildings in conservation areas, and emphasises the importance of how a building relates to its surroundings and of the quality of townscape.

Regional planning guidance (RPG) is also relevant and important. Under the new arrangements set out in PPG11 on Regional Planning, this is issued by the Secretary of State for the Environment, Transport and the Regions following a public examination into a draft submitted by the regional planning body. This body, working with other regional stakeholders is now responsible for preparing the draft guidance.

The more recent RPG has addressed design either by emphasising regionally important design issues to which local authorities should respond or by setting out a strategic framework for design policy.

Strategic planning guidance on specific topics has also been produced where necessary. An example is Strategic Planning Guidance for the River Thames, which sets out the Government's overall objectives for the river, and provides the strategic framework for land use planning along its banks.

Circular 5/94 *Planning Out Crime* provides advice on designing for community safety.

THE DEVELOPMENT PLAN

The 'development plan' provides an essential framework for guiding and controlling development. The development plan may comprise one or more types of plan depending on geographical location.

Among other things, the development plan:

• provides a vision for the area;

• identifies the main objectives to realise that vision;

• defines the local context of people and places;

• sets out the overall design policy framework (and other considerations) against which the local authority will assess development proposals;

• provides the policy foundation for supplementary planning guidance.

URBAN DESIGN AND THE DEVELOPMENT PLAN

Structure plans set out key strategic policies and provide a framework for local plans. Part I of a Unitary Development Plan (UDP) sets out a similarly strategic framework for the detailed proposals in Part II of the UDP. Most design policies will find their expression in the more detailed policies of local plans and UDP Part IIs. But local authorities, in developing the strategic framework within which the detailed policies of local plans and UDP Part IIs will be framed, should consider the importance of urban design in both influencing and helping to deliver the objectives shaped in the strategic plan.

VISION

Good plans include aims, objectives and targets. Collectively, these convey a vision of what is to be expected from the plan. A more detailed vision for an area can be developed through a local plan or UDP Part II and embrace both the sort of place the council is trying to achieve in terms of corporate objectives and of the physical form of development that would be most likely to achieve this. The plan should explain how these relate to the land use strategy that is brought forward: for example, how growth areas will be related to transport infrastructure and where centres will be developed.

The urban design objectives described earlier, or locally appropriate variations of them, can help to describe the sort of place it is hoped to create by physical development. Every plan should be different, because it reflects the unique circumstances of the particular place. Increasingly, the corporate plans of local authorities have sought their own distinctive emphasis. Recent examples include cities focusing on easy movement of people (Bristol, the legible city), innovation (Coventry, city of innovation), vitality (Leeds, the 24-hour city) and green issues (Leicester, the environment city). Such an emphasis should be reflected in the development plan's urban design objectives. For example, a place which values the protection of its heritage particularly highly would be likely to emphasise the objective of promoting distinctive character. Other places might decide on a different set of objectives to meet local conditions.

At the same time, any successful set of objectives is likely to be influenced by all the main matters embodied in the urban design objectives set out in this guide. The prompts to better urban design provide a useful starting point for writing design policies, tailored to local circumstances after carrying out context appraisals.

How the design policies are set out in the plan will depend on the emphasis that is appropriate locally. It may be convenient to set out urban design policies to reflect the appropriate design objectives. But in some plans it may be convenient to group design policies according to an aspect of development form (layout, scale, appearance and landscape) to which they relate, if that aspect is thought to be particularly important to the vision for the area.

The plan should explain how its urban design vision has been shaped by national policies and regional and local considerations. It should refer to any context appraisals that have been carried out and to the involvement of the public in them.

FROM OBJECTIVE TO POLICY

A policy or proposal that is likely to provide the basis for deciding planning applications, or for determining conditions to be attached to planning permissions, should be set out in the development plan, and may be augmented in supplementary planning guidance, such as design guides.

A plan's design policies, "should concentrate on guiding the overall scale, density, massing, height, landscape, layout and access of new development in relation to neighbouring buildings and the local area more generally" (PPG1). Too many plans cover all these factors in a single policy, which simply specifies that development must be 'acceptable' in terms of these matters, or that the scale, density, massing, height, landscape, layout and access of development must be 'appropriate'. Such policies are generally focussed on the objective of promoting or protecting an area's character, with the other urban design objectives too often neglected. Such phrases by themselves, however, offer no more guidance to a developer than is already contained in PPG1.

As well as setting out general design policies, a local plan or UDP Part II could include design policies relating to specific areas, specific sites or recurrent design issues. The plan could also explain how design issues are to be managed in the planning process, such as when and how supplementary planning guidance will be prepared. The plan should also explain what context appraisals have been carried out in developing policy.

43

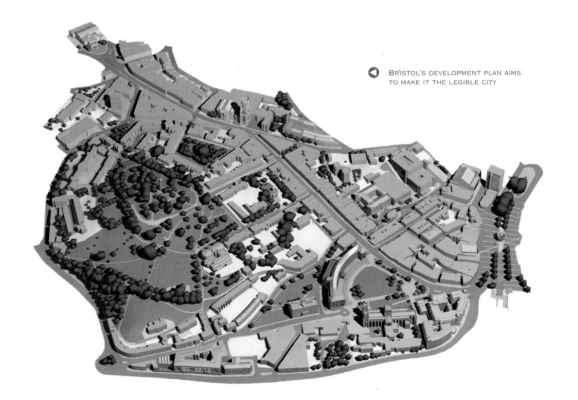

◀ BRISTOL'S DEVELOPMENT PLAN AIMS TO MAKE IT THE LEGIBLE CITY

The complete policy

A complete design policy in a local plan or UDP Part II would normally set out:

- a design aim, drawn from the urban design objectives and tailored to the local context;

- the criteria (considerations) against which planning applications would be considered; these criteria would make clear how the local authority would judge whether a proposed development would satisfactorily apply the principles embodied in the policy;

- reasoned justification, including an explanation of how the policy relates to other policies and objectives;

- an explanation of how the policy might be implemented (pointing, where appropriate, to supplementary planning guidance).

Good practice points

The following should be considered in writing plan policies:

- policies should make a meaningful contribution to planning decisions;

- policies should avoid unnecessary prescription or detail, be clearly expressed and be concise;

- the plan should guide planning applicants as to the council's design expectations in terms of the principles to be applied, not set out precisely how they should be met;

- policies should be monitored to determine how useful they are to development controllers and what impact they have on what is built.

WRITING GENERAL DESIGN POLICIES

A plan's general design policies provide the overall policy framework for design across the plan area, and they set the context for specific design policies. They also provide the basis for development control in circumstances where no more specific policies apply.

General design policies must be comprehensive (though not necessarily detailed) if they are to fulfil this role. In drafting general design policies, careful consideration should be given to the importance of each of the urban design objectives. The relative significance given to each objective will depend on the character of the plan area.

In some cases it may be appropriate to link design policies and conservation policies. A conservation policy may be a design policy which is applied in a particularly sensitive context.

Design policies should be written in a logical order that conveys to prospective applicants the thought processes they should go through in developing their design solutions. General design policies might be organised to reflect the local importance of certain objectives. The plan's policies should show how these objectives can be fulfilled. The prompts to thinking about urban design (section 2) tailored to the particular qualities and problems of the place could help. Detail that would not be decisive in determining a planning application should be avoided. It is more appropriate to include in supplementary planning guidance such detail as:

'Development should relate to the upper cornice line of St Mary's Church'

A general design policy

A local planning authority may for example wish to draft a general design policy on height.

Such a policy is likely to emphasise that consideration should be given to the scale, massing and height of proposed development in relation to that of adjoining buildings; the general pattern of heights in the area; and views, vistas and landmarks. The policy might be expanded, using the prompts (see Section 2, Character), by providing guidance on:

- the siting of landmark buildings or features so as to enhance existing views and vistas, and create new ones, helping people to find their way around;

- the contribution that development makes to a clearly defined and continuously enclosed public realm of routes and spaces;

- how public spaces could be protected from down-draughts from tall buildings as well as from lateral winds.

INTERCHANGES SHOULD BE DESIGNED TO ⬤
MAKE PUBLIC TRANSPORT EASY TO USE

ATTENTION TO DETAIL IS THE KEY TO ⬤
THE QUALITY OF THE PUBLIC REALM

WRITING SPECIFIC DESIGN POLICIES

Specific design policies relate to particular local conditions, and to the processes used locally to control development and prepare supplementary planning guidance. They should only be included in a plan to cover issues not already adequately dealt with through general design policies.

Types of specific design policies include:

- area-specific;

- site-specific;

- topic-based.

Area-specific policies

Area-specific policies can be needed for areas which make a highly significant contribution to shaping the distinct character of the plan area, or where guiding change is particularly important. Examples might include town centres, conservation areas, waterfronts, transport corridors, regeneration areas, the urban fringe, and areas of particular character or use. A local plan or UDP Part II should identify such areas if appropriate; making it clear which design policies will apply to specific areas; referring to any supplementary planning guidance that exists and explaining the intention to prepare urban design frameworks for these areas if that is the case.

Preparing design policies for a particular area will depend on an appraisal of its character, needs and development pressures, as understood both by planning and design professionals, and by local people. Such an appraisal must be rigorous, and based on collaboration and consultation, if it is to be an adequate basis for locally relevant design policies. Context appraisals should be analytical, not just descriptive.

45

46

An area-specific policy

A local planning authority may for example wish to draft an area-specific design policy for a town centre.

The issues are likely to be complex, so all the urban design objectives may apply. Ease of movement, quality of the public realm and continuity and enclosure may be the most important.

Such a policy is likely to emphasise that development should contribute to enhancing the focus of pedestrian movement and, perhaps, cultural activity in the town centre; should follow the historic building line, avoiding unnecessary setbacks; should provide active shopfronts along the main shopping street; and provide for residential uses above the shops.

The local authority may also wish to provide supplementary guidance on the use of materials and street furniture, making reference to the council's public space design guidelines, if any.

Site-specific policies

The plan should only include design policies which will apply to specific sites (avoiding unnecessary detail) if the design issue is of fundamental importance to the area.

Topic-based policies

A few design issues may be important enough to warrant including specific topic-based policies in the plan. These are likely to be elucidated in design guides. The plan should say what guides and other supplementary guidance have been prepared and will be prepared. Some common topics are types of development which are generally minor but also among the most common planning applications.

Possible subjects for such topic-based design policies include advertising and signage, house extensions, public art and shopfronts. Usually, the plan's general policies will cover these topics adequately without specific topic-based policies being required.

SUPPLEMENTARY PLANNING GUIDANCE

There are several ways in which local authorities can develop policies into clear design ideas for particular areas and sites, and in relation to specific planning and design issues. What follows are brief explanations of some of the tools a local authority can use to achieve the plan's policy aims and ensure that the plan itself is not encumbered with advisory material.

The tools considered here are urban design frameworks (which can be used to provide guidance for particular areas), development briefs (which provide guidance for particular sites) and design guides (which provide guidance on specific topics). Where this additional guidance is prepared as supplementary planning guidance (SPG) in the proper manner, it can carry significant weight when decisions are taken on planning applications.

PREPARING SUPPLEMENTARY PLANNING GUIDANCE

SPG can play a valuable role in supplementing the policies set out in the plan but it does not form part of the plan. It can provide helpful additional material for those preparing planning applications but should be issued separately.

SPG must not, however, be used to avoid subjecting to public scrutiny policies and proposals which should be included in the plan. Plan policies should not attempt to delegate the criteria for decisions on planning applications to SPG. Only the policies in the development plan can have special status in deciding planning applications but SPG may be taken into account as a material consideration. SPG should be prepared in consultation with the public, businesses and other interested parties, and their views should be taken into account before it is finalised. It should then be the subject of a council resolution to adopt it as supplementary guidance. On adoption, a statement of the consultation undertaken, the representations received and the council's response should be made available with each copy of the SPG (as an annex or seperately).

The urban design principle should be in the plan as policy. The various ways of achieving it should be in SPG. In order to keep the plan free of unnecessary detail any matter that does not need the authority of a plan policy should not be included in the plan.

SPG can be particularly useful in dealing with a matter that is:

- subject to frequent change for reasons outside the council's control;

- reliant on advice or documents produced by other bodies;

- advisory, rather than being a requirement.

As with development plan design policies, SPG is not interchangeable between one place and another. It must be based on context appraisals and should be the subject of public consultation. SPG will need to be monitored and reviewed in the light of experience (including planning appeals) and changes in policy and regulations. The method of monitoring and review should be considered from the start.

Council officers, developers and others may find SPG easier to use if they can become familiar with a consistent format and process of preparation.

Many readers of SPG will be unfamiliar with the specialised language and concepts of planning and design. Where they are used, they should be explained clearly in the text or in a glossary. Some local authorities make particular efforts to use clear language in all their publications. Birmingham City Council, for example, has a Plain Language Unit which helps all its departments make their policies, letters and other documents easy to understand. The Council assesses its documents for clarity and awards them a plain language logo where appropriate. The Plain English Campaign provides a similar service nationally.

It might be appropriate to publish information sheets or leaflets summarising SPG, especially where a specialist audience requires considerable technical detail while a more general message needs to be communicated to a wider audience.

Implementing supplementary planning guidance
SPG will be effective only if it develops the plan's principles into a set of design ideas appropriate both to economic conditions and to the site and its setting. But even the best ideas will be of no use if the document is left forgotten on a shelf.

The effectiveness of a design guide, development brief, or any other supplementary planning guidance will also depend on:

- the degree to which all relevant departments of the council are committed to it;

- the vigour with which council members and officers support it;

- the effectiveness of public participation in preparing it;

- how logically it is structured, how clearly it is written, and how well it is illustrated.

The following pages describe some of these types of SPG in more detail.

47

Example:

The relationship between a plan and its SPG

Hull CityPlan contains a single policy on 'Designing for telecommunications.' The policy reads: 'Telecommunications development will be allowed if the apparatus is sited and designed to minimise visual intrusion.'

This establishes that planning applications will be determined in the light of how visually intrusive the proposed apparatus would be. The local authority has published supplementary planning guidance to explain what this means. The city council's SPG Note 11 'Designing for satellite dishes' consists of two pages. It quotes other more general design policies from the CityPlan that are relevant to positioning satellite dishes; explains when planning permission is needed; and advises on how satellite dishes should be positioned.

The SPG suggests that views from streets and neighbouring properties should be respected, and that dishes should be placed where they are not obtrusive or seen against the sky; and it suggests seven positions where one should consider positioning a dish. These are illustrated in a diagram.

URBAN DESIGN FRAMEWORKS

Urban design frameworks provide guidance for areas undergoing change, or where growth and change needs to be promoted. A framework:

- explains and illustrates how development plan policies will be applied in an area;

- sets out comprehensive design principles for the area;

- links strategy to practical proposals;

- provides guidance for development control.

What a framework does

An urban design framework goes well beyond the level of detail appropriate for area-specific design policies in a plan. It draws on detailed area appraisals and sets out urban design principles. An urban design framework usually covers an area of which only some parts will be potential development sites. A framework goes beyond a traditional master plan, for example, by including an implementation strategy.

Birmingham City Council, has seen urban design frameworks as a logical conclusion of a process that started with the City Centre Strategy, subsequently incorporated into the Birmingham UDP. The Council sees them as a way of setting out the big picture before moving on to more detailed planning and urban design.

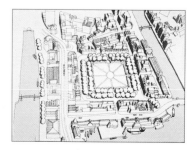

BRISTOL HAS USED URBAN DESIGN FRAMEWORKS TO GUIDE CHANGE IN MANY OF ITS INNER CITY AREAS

Urban design frameworks are also known by a variety of other names, including area development frameworks, urban design strategies, and planning and urban design frameworks.

An urban design framework can:

- create confidence, by:

  – evolving a shared vision and building consensus for action;

  – highlighting concerns and tackling particular problems and issues;

  – responding to changing local conditions and development pressures;

  – co-ordinating activity and resources, and harnessing local skills.

- manage change, by:

  – promoting high standards of design and providing a design framework for development control;

  – focusing on specific development opportunities and their phasing;

  – contributing to the plan preparation (and review) process where the existing plan does not provide an adequate policy context.

- provide a strategy for implementation, by:

  – providing the basis for bidding for public sector funds and securing private sector support;

  – providing an action plan and implementation programme.

Urban design frameworks and the development plan

Urban design frameworks are a means of applying plan policies (especially design policies) in particular areas where there is a need to guide and promote change. They can also form part of the framework for development control when used as supplementary planning guidance.

Urban design frameworks express design and planning concepts and proposals in two- and three-dimensional form through drawings, models and other techniques. They are relatively new design tools but are being used increasingly widely. There are many more opportunities to use them, but there is no merit in providing comprehensive coverage where there is no special need. Where they are prepared the aim should be to create the basis for a dialogue with developers and anyone else interested in an area, not to set out a rigid structure for what must happen.

Urban design frameworks are generally initiated and prepared by local authorities, landowners or developers, partnerships, or regeneration agencies.

Where a framework is used

An urban design framework can help frame the context for more detailed development briefs for specific sites within an area. In a case where several sites in an area are available for development, it can provide a strategy for preparing the briefs in a way that will ensure that developments will complement rather than compete with each other.

AN URBAN DESIGN FRAMEWORK FOR PART OF WORCESTER CITY CENTRE

49

From policy to guidance

An urban design framework enables the design of the whole or parts of complex urban environments to be dealt with in a comprehensive and connected way. All aspects of development form need to be considered when developing area-based strategies.

Urban design frameworks are appropriate in a variety of settings:

- city-wide as a means of understanding the dynamics of a place;

- neighbourhoods and districts including areas of distinctive character, use and perceived identity;

- urban quarters with mixed uses including housing, arts, culture and entertainment areas;

- regeneration areas including brownfield sites, housing and industrial estates;

- town and city centres including guidance for a full range of revitalisation initiatives;

- town extensions including new housing and industrial developments;

- villages by expanding on village design statements, as promoted by the Countryside Agency;

- transport corridors which focus on major routes on road, rail and river corridors;

- special policy areas such as waterfronts, special landscape and conservation areas.

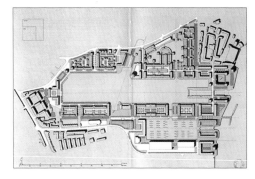

THE LONDON DOCKLANDS DEVELOPMENT CORPORATION SUCCESSFULLY USED AN URBAN DESIGN-LED APPROACH TO MARKETING AND DEVELOPING GREENLAND DOCK

Regeneration areas

In this example a local planning authority wants to promote a regeneration initiative for a large managed-workspace and residential complex, reusing its historic industrial buildings and developing a number of large derelict sites.

Important design objectives are likely to be promoting character, ease of movement, adaptability and diversity. Improving the public realm could also help to promote positive change. In drafting design policy and SPG thought should be given to how the various aspects of form deliver the important objectives, and in particular, how:

- the proposed urban structure responds to the existing settlement pattern and creates a clear hierarchy of routes and spaces;

- subdividing large sites into development blocks and sites can encourage mixed uses;

- density guidelines can be framed to take full advantage of accessibility to local public transport;

- the height of new buildings relates to the existing scale of development in the area, avoiding overshadowing existing residential areas;

- the massing of new development respects the scale and building forms of the historic industrial buildings;

- new development can be successfully integrated into the landscape.

Section 2 gives a number of prompts to thinking about urban design which cover these design issues. They could be used to help prepare design policy and SPG.

This page sets out the basis of an urban design framework. Its approach uses the objectives of urban design to shape urban form and generate activity. The framework could be for either a town centre or an area requiring new development or regeneration.

1
An urban design framework for an inner city site highlights the constraints and opportunities…

5
…focuses civic and community building onto major routes and spaces…

2
…identifies the opportunities for an integrated network of public transport…

6
…promotes frontage development and a range of complementary uses on busy streets…

3
…relates opportunities for increased density to public transport accessibility…

7
…establishes a pattern of local streets and blocks which are clearly contained and enclosed…

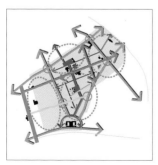

4
…draws out a hierarchy of connected routes and spaces that link well into transport routes…

8
…and brings forward guidance (or design codes) on issues such as scale (height and massing) and the public realm.

52

Example:

Initiating urban design frameworks
in Birmingham and Coventry

A wide range of approaches has been used to
initiate urban design frameworks. Birmingham
and Coventry provide two examples.

At the first event of Birmingham's Highbury Initiative,
in 1988, over a period of 48 hours international
specialists from a variety of disciplines worked with
people who knew the city intimately on the
opportunities of Birmingham city centre. Eighteen
months later a second event brought together
many of the same people to review progress.

The initiative had a significant influence on city
centre policy and action on planning and design,
leading to the preparation of the City Centre
Design Strategy and Birmingham's quarter
framework plans. The Highbury Initiative shows
how bringing in outsiders can help to generate
new ideas at the start of the process.

The City of Coventry has embarked on a
comprehensive urban design-led strategy to
guide the future of the whole city. The aims are
to promote good design particularly in the city
centre, along transport corridors and in areas of
special character. Many of the concerns outlined
in Section 2 have been addressed in the review
of Coventry's Unitary Development Plan.
The process has involved councillors, council
officers, residents and other stakeholders coming
together to define their ambitions for the city.
This has led to a number of regeneration
initiatives, including a proposal to downgrade
part of the raised inner ringway and reinstate
links with surrounding areas.

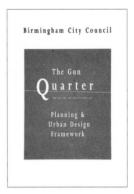

Birmingham City Council

The Gun
Quarter

Planning &
Urban Design
Framework

⬤ BIRMINGHAM HAS PREPARED A SERIES OF
URBAN DESIGN FRAMEWORKS TO GUIDE
THE DEVELOPMENT OF URBAN QUARTERS

Example:

The Piggeries Housing Scheme, Frome

The Piggeries is the product of dedicated efforts
by Mendip District Council to turn round a
derelict part of Frome blighted by major road
proposals. Through land assembly and a clear
urban design philosophy the council has fostered
a re-development that provides an attractive
living environment sensitive to its surroundings.
The establishment of a multi-disciplinary project
group early on in the process was crucial to
the scheme's success, as was the involvement
of the local community.

⬤ ONE OF THE DESIGN PRINCIPLES WAS TO RETAIN THE
EXISTING FOOTPATH NETWORK

DEVELOPMENT BRIEFS

A development brief sets out in detail how the plan's policies should be implemented on a specific site.

A brief:

- expresses a set of coherent development principles based on analysis of the planning context;

- is prepared for a site of significant size, sensitivity or complexity;

- minimises uncertainty and improves efficiency of the planning and development process;

- can be used to promote development by identifying constraints, providing realistic ideas and stimulating interest in mixed uses and high standards of design.

What a brief does

A development brief provides clear guidance on how a site should be developed. It is potentially one of the most effective means of articulating the design principles for a site and implementing design (and other planning) policies.

Development briefs are also known by a variety of other names, including planning briefs, design briefs and site development frameworks. There are no standard definitions as to what they should include, further advice is provided in *Planning and Development Briefs: a guide to better practice*. As design is an integral part of planning, there is no need for separate planning briefs and design briefs.

The outcome of the design and planning process on a particular site will be determined and influenced by policies and standards; market conditions; the local context; and the approach of designers and project managers. A brief can help to achieve a balance between these and to resolve potential conflicts.

A development brief will not be required if the development plan and any existing SPG provide adequate guidance for any developer, and if there is no need to establish a set of urban design ideas and principles for the site. If a development brief is to be worth preparing, it must aim to secure a higher standard of development than would have been achieved without it.

What a brief contains

A development brief:

- provides a clear statement of why the brief has been prepared and what it seeks to achieve;

- shows (in words, diagrams, photographs and drawings) how the plan's design policies could be applied on the site;

- provides the basic area and site appraisal that is an essential requirement for good design;

- sets out design objectives for the site, shows the first stages of urban design analysis and expresses initial urban design ideas;

- conveys the local authority's hopes and expectations, persuades developers of what the site has to offer, and inspires them to design and plan for the highest possible standards;

- includes a summary of the consultation undertaken and the authority's response to the issues raised.

53

A development brief's requirements should be specific, and expressed in a way which will make it possible to assess the degree to which a subsequent proposal reflects the brief. It may be useful for the brief to include a checklist of the criteria which would be used. Applicants should explain in their planning application design statement how they have responded to any brief.

The planning and design considerations within a brief should be more than just a list of the relevant design policies, but reflect thinking as to how those policies should be applied in the light of the type of development that seems most economically feasible as well as the local context.

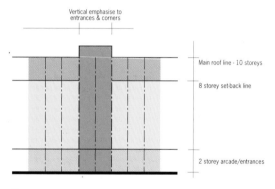

Vertical emphasise to
entrances & corners

Main roof line - 10 storeys

8 storey set-back line

2 storey arcade/entrances

A DEVELOPMENT BRIEF CAN DESCRIBE BUILDING ASPECTS SUCH AS HEIGHT, SETBACKS, FACADE ARTICULATION AND TREATMENT OF THE GROUND FLOOR

From policy to guidance

How elaborate a brief should be (and what level of resources its preparation will require) will depend on the scale, sensitivity and complexity of the site. At the simplest, a brief for a small infill site may require no more than straight-forward guidance about such matters as height, access, the building line and materials, and consultation with neighbours.

On large housing or brownfield sites requiring an orderly approach to phased development, the emphasis is likely to be on layout, density and massing. Landscape is likely to be particularly important on greenfield sites, with topography,

ecology, watersheds and boundaries needing careful attention. A development brief for a large site will have many of the characteristics of an urban design framework, but it will be tailored to such detailed issues as density, access and circulation requirements, relationships to adjacent development, and new landscape.

On smaller sites within established urban areas where any new form of development will have a marked effect on the existing context (such as in or near conservation areas or within the city centre) the emphasis is likely to be on massing and appearance. Thought needs to be given to how new development will relate to the existing in terms of height and massing as well as in details and materials. The issues of maintaining continuous building lines and relationships with the street will be of prime importance. Attention will also need to be given to the scope for adaptive reuse of retained buildings both to enhance and to maintain the character of the area.

Development briefs may also be needed where a coordinated approach through preparing a development strategy can overcome complex issues or constraints involved in developing a site.

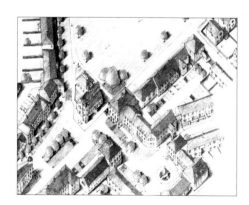

THIS BRIEF SHOWS HOW LAYOUT AND MASSING CAN INTEGRATE DEVELOPMENT INTO ITS SURROUNDINGS

Large sites

In this example an extension to a small town is contemplated.

In developing design guidance for the proposed development, the objectives of promoting character, continuity and enclosure and accessibility may well be the most important. In drafting design policy and SPG, thought should be given to how the development will be laid out in response to the site's land form and character. It is likely that the design policy would emphasise that (i) the layout and landscape design of development should reinforce a sense of place; (ii) the landscape treatment of the site and urban edges should place particular emphasis on how the development relates to its landscape setting.

The design policy could be expanded through SPG to show:

- how the development could respond to the natural features of the site;

- the benefits of planting species that are locally common;

- how structure planting and shelter belts could be created on the rural boundaries of the site to provide a clearly defined urban edge;

- the way the various elements of the street scene could contribute to the identity of the place, including sculpture, lighting, railings, litter bins, paving, hard landscape, seating, bollards, kiosks, cycle racks, signage and water features.

The prompts to thinking about urban design in Section 2 would be a useful starting point for informing the preparation of the guidance. Detailed site appraisals would help in understanding the nature and complexity of the site, enabling more sensitive guidance to be developed.

Preparing a brief

Most briefs are prepared by local authorities, but landowners, developers, regeneration partnerships, and business and community organisations can also prepare them, preferably in consultation with the council.

A wide range of people will usually need to be involved in preparing the brief. An effective brief may need the involvement of landowners and developers to provide information on economic conditions, and local people and interest groups to highlight values, needs, expectations and live issues. Representatives of interests that might later want to influence a planning application should be consulted or involved in preparing the brief. All the relevant departments and disciplines should be represented on the local authority's team.

Preparing a development brief calls for design skills. These will be needed in particular in appraising the site in relation to everything that might be relevant to the form and appearance of buildings and spaces; and in drawing up and illustrating a series of site-specific design principles.

A local authority which does not have sufficient in-house design expertise to prepare a development brief itself might:

- commission consultants to advise on design;

- rely on another organisation (such as a developer) to prepare the brief;

- collaborate with a voluntary organisation.

In any case the council will need to have sufficient design expertise to manage the consultants effectively, or to assess the design element (that is, everything that might be relevant to the physical form of buildings and spaces) of the brief.

One district council's procedure for preparing development briefs:

- a lead officer convenes a multi-disciplinary team;

- all interested bodies are informed that the brief is to be prepared;

- an initial site meeting is held to which the following are invited: chairman of development committee, chairman and vice chairman of area planning sub-committee, ward councillor(s), chairman of town/parish council, site owner(s), developer, representative of county surveyor, officers preparing the brief and other interested parties;

- a first draft and site appraisal plan are prepared and sent to councillors; working drawings, illustrations or indicative layouts may be prepared to test the emerging thoughts on development options against the brief's objectives, but these will not appear in subsequent drafts (so as not to stifle originality);

- the brief is reconsidered in the light of councillors' responses;

- a second draft is sent to town/parish council meeting, site owner/agent and other consultees and the need for further public involvement considered;

- the final brief is written for approval by the council;

- the brief is circulated widely.

Good practice points

- multi-disciplinary team

- councillors are involved at an early stage

- brief is well publicised and circulated widely

THE DRAWINGS IN A BRIEF SHOULD NOT GO BEYOND WHAT IS NEEDED TO ILLUSTRATE THE PLANNING AND DESIGN PRINCIPLES

A brief can be illustrated by concept diagrams, building envelope guidelines (diagrams with dimensions) and three-dimensional sketches of building forms and spaces. Such drawings should not go beyond what is required to explain the application of the principles.

A design brief should communicate strong design ideas, without actually designing buildings or layouts. Those who prepare briefs are sometimes tempted to design a building or buildings which would conform to the principles, and to include the fully worked-up drawings in the brief. This may confuse potential developers, who will not easily be able to tell which aspects of the drawings illustrate the application of the principles, and which have been included merely to enhance the drawings' appearance. Prescriptive design and any suggestion of a particular style should be avoided.

Developer-initiated briefs

The process followed by one district council when a developer (or landowner) initiates a development brief for housing:

Stage 1: the appraisal

- policy context defined and forwarded to applicant;

- consultation undertaken with public authorities and responses forwarded to the developer before the brief is drafted;

- developer appraises physical character of the site;

- consultation with the local community, responses appraised by the developer;

- housing market study largely undertaken by the developer, with input by the local authority on affordable housing.

Stage 2: the development brief

- developer compiles details of site constraints and opportunities;

- applicant compiles development options;

- all appraisals and briefs approved by the local authority. If a brief submitted by a developer is refused, the developer can negotiate further and make a revised submission, or pursue an application for planning permission.

Good practice points

- the respective roles of the council and the developer, and the role of negotiation, are made clear from the start;

- the council approves the developer's appraisals, providing an increasing degree of certainty throughout the process; the council will seek to negotiate with the developer where it feels there are omissions or differences of interpretation.

DESIGN GUIDES

A design guide provides detailed guidance on how specific types of development can be carried out in accordance with a plan's design policies. A guide:

- elucidates and exemplifies a set of design principles relating to that topic;

- identifies common design failings and helps to avoid them;

- provides a basis for consistency in the local authority's dealings with planning applicants and a basis for negotiation;

- enables a local authority to communicate its commitment to design both internally and to everyone involved in the development process;

- some design guides, on satellite dishes for example, may relate to a single policy. Others, on complex subjects such as mixed-use development, will relate to a number of policies.

⊙

THE DESIGN OF SHOPFRONTS IS THE MOST COMMON TOPIC FOR GUIDELINES

⊙ AN EXTENSION REFLECTING THE FORM OF THE ORIGINAL HOUSE

What a design guide does

Design guides are among the most common mechanisms used by local authorities (and others) to influence the design of development. The most successful guides have the committed support of all the relevant council officers and planning committee members, and are clearly understood by local developers, architects and other users.

Design guides can inspire innovative design appropriate to its context; raise standards of a particular type of development where problems have been identified; and provide answers to questions frequently asked by applicants.

Design guides enable local authorities to guide development in relation to particular design issues and type of development, elucidating the design policies in the development plan. Producing a design guide can be an effective use of a council's design skills, in cases where officers find themselves repeatedly giving the same advice.

What a design guide contains

A well-prepared design guide will usually include:

- the purpose of the guide;

- information on how to use the guide and who produced it;

- an account of consultation on the guide and the authority's response;

- current status (draft for consultation, for example) and eventual status (SPG, for example);

- an explanation of the policy context, how the guide relates to plan policies, national guidance, other design guides, development briefs, and relevant initiatives such as any relating to town centre management, security or conservation;

- an explanation of what context appraisals the guide is based on, and a summary of what they showed;

- design guidance, illustrating the design policies in the development plan through a set of design principles relating to the specific topic and the local context;

- illustrations, photographs and plans (with captions, except where the illustration is included purely to make the document attractive);

- information on when planning permission is required and submission requirements;

- a glossary (unless all specialised terms are explained where they appear in the text);

- references to further information;

- grants available (if relevant);

- contacts in the local authority and other organisations;

- details of specialist manufacturers, contractors and advisors (on crime prevention, for example) where appropriate.

From policy to guidance

Design guides deal with a wide range of design and development control topics. Some cover a limited number of aspects of form and only some of the objectives.

Design guides for buildings – design guides can cover such topics as shopfronts, building extensions and signs, dealing largely with the appearance (details and materials) and scale (massing). In a guide on shopfronts, for example, the objectives of promoting character and ease of understanding are likely to be the most important.

Streetscape and landscape design manuals – design guides on routes and spaces cover topics such as public space, cycling, landscape, lighting and works of art. The emphasis is on promoting character, quality of the public realm, ease of movement and ease of understanding. Design guides on landscape cover topics such as nature conservation, planting, hydrology and land form. The emphasis is on promoting character.

Design guides for specific uses – design guides should avoid covering types of development (such as residential, leisure, retail or industrial) in ways which may encourage single-use development. Residential design guides can help to raise the standards of housing design and layout but care must be taken to encourage diversity and integration with other land uses. There is sometimes a case for replacing guides for specific uses with neighbourhood, district and city development guides.

Neighbourhood, district and city development guides – some design guides relate to areas such as neighbourhoods, parts of or whole cities and towns (such as the Manchester Development Guide). The guidance may well cover all the objectives outlined in Section 2 (as modified by the local context). Such guides can play a valuable role in guiding development, promoting mixed use, acting as vision documents, stimulating regeneration and contributing to city marketing.

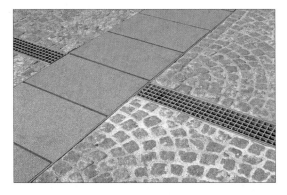

⬤ DESIGN GUIDES FOR PUBLIC SPACE CAN HELP INSPIRE DEVELOPMENT WHICH PROMOTES OBJECTIVES SUCH AS CHARACTER AND QUALITY OF THE PUBLIC REALM

Countryside design summaries – this is SPG prepared by a local authority to encourage a more regionally and locally based approach to design and planning.

Village design statements – these are advisory documents, usually produced by village communities, showing how development can be carried out in harmony with the village and its setting. These statements can be adopted as SPG. The use of village design statements is promoted by the Countryside Agency.

Neighbourhood design guide

In this example a district council wants to promote better housing design and layout through a neighbourhood design guide aimed at volume housebuilders.

Many of the sites identified for development in its local plan are next to existing residential areas. This suggests it is important to integrate the new with the old.

Most objectives and aspects of form are likely to be relevant in preparing such a design guide. The layout of the area is particularly important. For sites well-connected to public transport, the council may also want to specify a minimum development density and a mix of uses. Height and massing will also need to be carefully considered. The guide might explain how landscaping and design detail such as the use of appropriate materials can promote local character and a high quality of public realm.

Preparing a design guide
Most design guides are produced by local authorities, but they are also produced by regeneration agencies and partnerships (such as Hulme Regeneration) or housing associations (such as the Guinness Trust).

Preparing a design guide is likely to involve the local community and several parts of the council (such as development control, design and conservation, local plan, building regulations, highways, estates and community liaison).

It will usually be appropriate for other stakeholders to be involved in the preparation, such as the Chamber of Commerce, other trade associations, the local branch of the RIBA, amenity and interest groups, civic societies, design and conservation advisory panels, and nearby local authorities.

Presentation

It is helpful:

- to decide whether the guide is to be sent out (in whole or part) with planning application forms, and design it (in terms of weight and cost, for example) accordingly;

- to produce the guide in two parts (a technical document and a popular summary) where appropriate;

- if the guide is to be copied in parts for sending to planning applicants, to ensure it is written so that each part is self-sufficient;

- to specify an appropriate quality of production to ensure that circulation is not limited by an excessive price (or cost of free distribution);

- to produce worksheets and checklists (on matters such as typical details, materials and schedules), as appropriate, to supplement the guide.

However well it is conceived, structured and written, the extent to which a design guide is read, understood and used will depend a good deal on how it is presented graphically. In the best design guides the structure is made clear by the appropriate use of headlines, type and size of text. Headlines and captions make it possible to skim through the guide and get

a clear idea of the structure and contents, before going back to read it or use it for reference.

Illustrations, photographs and plans which do not have a purpose, may have a place as a means of making the guide look attractive, breaking up the text, or through adding to the general impression that is being made. But they will do little or nothing to convey information or reinforce the text. Most illustrations, photographs and plans without captions stating the point they are intended to make do not have a useful purpose.

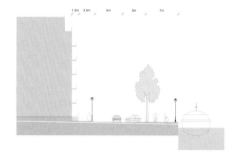

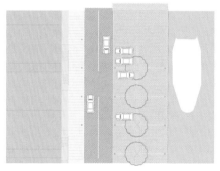

△ ILLUSTRATIONS ARE OFTEN THE KEY TO AN EFFECTIVE DESIGN GUIDE

Promotion

A design guide is only effective if it is seen and used. Guides can be:

- put on display in the planning department and other council offices;

- put on display in public libraries;

- given to planning applicants at pre-planning application meetings;

- sent out with forms about a grant scheme;

- sent out with planning application forms, where appropriate (either the whole guide, relevant parts of it, or a leaflet about it);

- sent out by council officers (as a whole and with specific sections copied) in response to enquiries;

- used in negotiations;

- promoted through demonstration projects;

- referred to in the development plan and other documents;

- referred to in the local authority's planning handbook and on planning application forms, where appropriate.

Using the guide

It is important that everyone, including development control officers and planning committee members, in a position to apply its principles is committed to the guide. This can be secured by:

- holding internal seminars and continuing professional development (CPD) talks with council members and officers;

- showing (by way of publications or visits) how the guide has led to higher standards of design;

- holding seminars with potential users of the guide, including people who regularly submit planning applications, as agents for householders and developers.

Instant results should not be expected. The benefits will be seen when development control officers and users of the guide get used to it and absorb the principles it embodies. The application of design guides will need to be complemented by skilled negotiation and appropriate consultation.

DEVELOPMENT CONTROL

The development control process is an essential item in the planning toolkit. How it is used determines whether the design policies in development plans and supplementary planning guidance are respected and applied. Even the most thoroughly developed design policies will achieve next to nothing if they are ignored in the development control process. The next section considers how a planning application should be handled if a good design result is to be achieved.

It is the statutory responsibility of council members and officers to see that development proposals are determined in accordance with the objectives and principles expressed in the development plan, including those relating to design "unless material considerations indicate otherwise". To achieve this requires a proper understanding of these principles, and the skill to assess the design quality of projects and negotiate improvements where necessary.

Through published plans and guidance, potential applicants should be in a position to understand what development is likely to be acceptable to the local authority. An understanding and helpful approach from development control officers should help applicants resolve conflicts and meet the requirements of the statutory procedures, ensuring that the development control process proceeds effectively and efficiently.

THE PRE-APPLICATION STAGE

Applicants want a favourable decision quickly. The fastest approvals can be given when the applicant brings forward a high quality proposal. This is more likely to happen if the applicant has discussed the proposal with planning officers before submitting the application, and has consulted adjoining owners and other interested parties.

The aim should be to expose any potential conflicts arising from a development proposal in the early stages of the design process. Resolving these conflicts early helps to avoid confrontation and polarised attitudes during the later, formal stages of the application. Insufficient preparatory work before submitting a planning application can lead to time-consuming delays later.

It should be evident to the applicant from the outset that the local authority is committed to a high standard of design. Formal expressions of policy can be reinforced in subtle ways, for example by a well-designed and attractive reception area in the council offices, with illustrations of well-designed projects and details about local design initiatives.

The negotiation process

Negotiations between an applicant and local authority should aim to be effective and successful for both parties. It is important at the outset that both parties are clear about their overall objectives and explicit about likely sticking points. This will help the applicant to appreciate the relative weight of different council policies and the most important design considerations. It will also help the planning officer understand the economic and market conditions relating to a particular development proposal. The planner will be better able to judge whether the application is a planning exercise to establish the value of a site for marketing purposes, or a genuine development proposal.

The basis for discussions on design will have been set by the policies in the development plan and any SPG. It is important at the beginning of these discussions to concentrate on the most important urban design considerations, such as the location of the proposed building(s) on the site, their height and massing, their relationship to site boundaries and adjoining properties, access to the site and circulation within it. Architectural detail is unlikely to be an issue at this stage.

In some cases the applicant's intentions and the council's design policies will be incompatible. If so, it may be necessary to terminate discussions and indicate that, if pressed to a conclusion, the application would be recommended for refusal. It is bad practice to continue beyond this point if the likely result is a poor compromise where, in view of the time they have spent together in negotiations, the planning officer feels obliged to support the applicant by recommending a mediocre scheme to the planning committee. Neither party may be happy with the outcome. If the committee refuses the application, the applicant may feel misled and resent the time that has been wasted.

Offering advice

The planning officer is often asked to provide a design solution, particularly where the applicant has not appointed an architect. Even some architects will invite a planning officer to draw an alternative layout or building elevation. Planning officers should be highly circumspect in these situations. It may be more appropriate to advise the applicant to employ a qualified designer who will have the time to understand the brief properly and provide a professional service. Design quality does not rest solely on the initial design and the planning consent, but on the development processes that follow. A building project should receive the appropriate level of design effort and expertise throughout its duration.

Design guidance offered during a negotiation (beyond that available in published documents) is best given by a qualified designer – an architect, landscape architect or urban designer. It is important that a local planning authority employs staff with professional design training, or can draw on these skills through alternative arrangements.

Example:

Designing the new Hulme, Manchester

The new Hulme is a return to streets, squares and civic spaces. Community involvement in the planning, design and development process has been extensive and is reflected in the 'Hulme Guide to Development' which provided the design guidance for the area. Local people wanted to see traditional street patterns and a community with a mix of housing and facilities. The new Hulme responds to these aspirations and backed by a substantial programme of economic and social change the community's prospects have been turned round.

△ NEW LOOK HULME PROMPTED BY DESIGN GUIDANCE AND THE VIEWS OF RESIDENTS

△ THE OLD HULME

MAKING THE TRANSFORMATION ▽

 △ HULME ARCH BRIDGE    ▽ A MIXED USE HOUSING CO-OPERATIVE SCHEME

63

64

Example:

Bede Island North, Leicester

Bede Island has been turned from an eyesore on the edge of Leicester's City Centre into an attractive and vibrant place to live, work and play. The mixed use development is based firmly on good design principles and grew from a planning brief that set out clear requirements for the uses, form and layout to be achieved. The transformation represents the hard work of a City Challenge partnership working closely with its local community.

A FORMER PUMP HOUSE CONVERTED INTO A PUBLIC HOUSE FORMS ONE SIDE OF THE SQUARE. THE TOWER IS A LOCAL LANDMARK

AXONOMETRIC SKETCH OF BEDE ISLAND SHOWING THE PUBLIC SQUARE AT THE HEART OF THE COMMUNITY

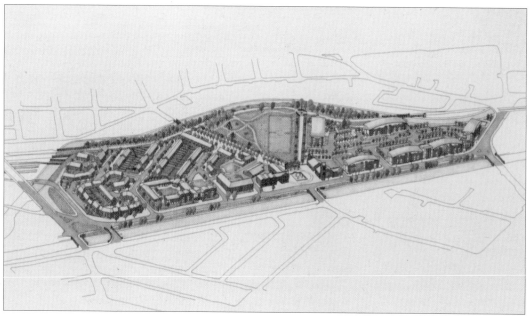

Pre-application design statements

A pre-application design statement can be made by a developer to explain the design principles on which a development proposal is based, and how these will be reflected in its layout, density, scale, landscape and visual appearance. It can explain how these principles were evolved from the relevant policy, site and area appraisal, and consultation. The statement enables the local authority to give an initial response to the main issues raised by the proposal.

Such a design statement can be an effective and flexible mechanism for structuring the design and planning process, in the case of a site which is not the subject of a development brief. The statement can:

- enable the local authority to be proactive;

- highlight and resolve potential conflict at an early stage;

- ensure that the developer has as much certainty as possible as the design process progresses, reducing the likelihood of unexpected delays, abortive work and unnecessary expense;

- create the conditions for good design;

- structure the design and planning process;

- facilitate the process of pre-application negotiations between developer and planners;

- provide a basis for later evaluating the development proposal;

- provide a basis for public participation, as appropriate.

The pre-application design statement might outline:

- the policy background, identifying all relevant policies, development briefs, design guides, standards and regulations;

- the context, including a site and area appraisal (illustrated with diagrams), summaries of relevant studies, and reports of any relevant consultations;

- feasibility factors, including summaries of economic and market conditions (subject to the need for commercial confidentiality);

- the design and project management approach. This will include an outline of the various stages of the design process (for example: site and area appraisal, design workshops, design panels, urban design and building design) and a description of the design skills which will be employed at each stage;

- the design principles which have been formulated in response to the policy background, the site and its settings and the purpose of the development, and an outline of how these will be reflected in the development's layout, density, scale, landscape and visual appearance;

- a programme of meetings with the local authority and other bodies;

- a proposed programme of participation and consultation. The appropriate level of consultation will depend on the degree to which consultation has already been carried out in the preparation of any relevant development briefs or design guides and on statutory requirements.

The level of detail required will depend on the scale and sensitivity of the development. A statement relating to an application to build or alter a single house can be brief and straightforward. Describing the context, for example, might involve a simple sketch of the house and the buildings on each side of it, and a short description of the general character of the street. The design statement for a development on a large and sensitive site would need to be detailed and comprehensive.

Preparing the statement

In the case of a potential development of significant size or sensitivity, a local authority which takes a proactive approach will discuss with the developer the intended stages of the design process, and set out the roles and responsibilities of the main players. At an early meeting the developer and the council may agree that the developer will produce a pre-application design statement.

The local authority will respond to the design statement as part of the process of negotiation, helping the developer to progress the proposal, and confirming the council's design expectations. The developer may revise the design statement in the light of the local authority's response. The revised statement may be referred to in assessing the subsequent planning application.

PLANNING APPLICATION STAGE

A planning application should take the local planning authority through the thought processes that have gone into the design. It should be submitted in a form that demonstrates how the proposal responds to the site, the locality and the policy context.

Planning application design statements

As laid down in PPG1, applicants for planning permission should provide a written statement setting out the design principles they have adopted in relation to the site and its wider context. This helps in assessing the application against design policies, and it requires applicants to think about design in an analytical and positive way.

A design statement submitted with planning applications should:

- explain the design principles and design concept;

- outline how these are reflected in the development's layout, density, scale, visual appearance and landscape;

- explain how the design relates to its site and wider area (through a full site and area appraisal where appropriate), and to the purpose of the proposed development;

- explain how the development will meet the local authority's urban design objectives (and its other planning policies);

- include a popular summary where this would be of value in public consultation.

Planning application design statements are appropriate for even the smallest and most uncontroversial development proposals, as together these have an enormous impact on the environment. In such cases only a brief statement explaining the design approach (appropriately illustrated) is likely to be necessary.

A written design statement should be illustrated, as appropriate, by:

- plans and elevations;

- photographs of the site and its surroundings;

- other illustrations, such as perspectives.

Other information to support a planning application
'Checklist 2' in the appendices points to the material to be submitted with a planning application to enable the design to be properly assessed.

It is important that plans and illustrations submitted with planning applications should be suitable for their purpose. Technical production drawings contain information which is superfluous to the planning process. They are unlikely to convey the character of the design in a way that is helpful to the officers and members assessing it for the local authority. Coloured plans may be more easily understood, and three-dimensional drawings and architectural models are particularly helpful. Perspectives must be accurate (many planning authorities are mistrustful of 'artists impressions', which have sometimes been deliberately misleading) and drawn from a viewpoint which is relevant (usually from a significant public location). Eye-level for the perspective should normally be two metres above ground level, not that of a bird in flight.

Drawings of elevations should extend some way beyond site boundaries to show the relationship of the proposal to neighbouring buildings. Long street elevations showing a proposal in its context are particularly helpful. Again, drawings must be accurate.

THE PLANNING DECISION

Having established that a development proposal is likely to be acceptable in relation to broad considerations of land-use and traffic generation, the design aspects should be addressed at an early stage. The key urban design issues need to be identified against the background of design policies and any specific site briefing.

Seeking qualified advice

Qualified designers can be scarce in local planning departments, where this is the case it is important that their time is focused on important schemes and issues. Their contribution may be made in a number of ways, including the setting up of design review panels or design surgeries to which development control officers bring cases for a specialist view. Whether such arrangements are made or not, all development control staff must understand the design policies in the development plan and SPG, be able to recognise the relevant issues and know when it is appropriate to seek specialist advice.

Whenever possible a qualified designer should join the council's development control officer in any significant discussions about design with applicants

or their architects. Other professionals who play a role in the development control process can have an influence on design quality, for better or worse. This is particularly true of highway engineers. It is important to involve them in any urban design training that is carried out within the local authority to ensure that their approach is complementary to that of the planning staff. Their contribution to development control casework should be as members of a team, rather than as consultees at arm's length.

Checklists can be useful in ensuring that all the relevant design issues have been considered. They can help to establish a routine within the planning control process that gives proper attention to design quality.

Independent assessments

For major applications, and where it does not have adequate staff design skills for a particular evaluation, a local authority may wish to commission an independent design assessment.

Such an assessment can be carried out by consultants, by another local authority, or by some other agency. It may be appropriate for the developer to meet all or part of the cost of the assessment. Indeed the developer may sometimes opt to commission an independent assessment (from an advisor respected by the local authority) to form part of the design submission at planning application stage or following a period of negotiation.

An independent design assessment can:

- provide a local authority with a basis for more informed decision-making;

- give a developer independent design advice;

- provide the basis for rejecting a design of poor quality;

- complement other assessments, such as those on retail, transport and environmental impacts.

Design advisory panels

A number of local authorities use independent design advisory panels (also known as architectural advisory panels) to help them assess the design aspects of planning applications. Some panels meet frequently to consider relevant items on the planning committee agenda. Others become involved only where there is a dispute between an architect or designer and a planning officer, which cannot otherwise be resolved.

The skills and experience of a design advisory panel can be more fully used by involving it at an earlier stage in the planning process, such as in the preparation of design policies, development briefs and design guides.

The use of advisory panels is supported by both the Royal Institute of British Architects (RIBA) and the Royal Town Planning Institute (RTPI). The RIBA publishes a Practice Guidance Note on architects' advisory panels, including model terms of reference and a specimen form of report. Some panels consist only of architects, while others benefit from a much wider range of design advice. The membership of a panel should not produce the result that a group of local architects are commenting on each other's work.

The planning decision and committee process

In the case of a detailed planning application, the officer's report to committee should draw from the applicant's design statement and where appropriate attach it, or a summary of it, as an appendix. The report should also consider and evaluate the main design issues. Sometimes it will be possible to accept a proposal in principle while certain design details remain to be resolved. A conditional approval can then be granted, allowing details of materials, landscaping, boundary treatments or even the elevation treatment of all or part of a building to be approved later. The fundamental urban design principles of a scheme should not, however be relegated for later consideration. They must be acceptable at the time any consent is granted.

▲ THE ADAPTABILITY OF THIS BUILDING IN NEWCASTLE-UPON-TYNE HAS ENABLED IT TO BE CONVERTED FROM WAREHOUSES TO OFFICES

It is important that members of the planning committee can see proper and full evidence of the design quality of proposals which they are being recommended to approve. Architectural models and reliable and accurate perspective drawings are invaluable. (With advances in information technology it can be expected that in the future committees will be able to see computerised simulations of journeys around and through proposed buildings. They will be able to select viewpoints for computer-generated three-dimensional images of buildings.)

It is also helpful for someone with design training to be on hand at the committee to explain and discuss design issues, and respond to members' questions and suggestions.

While committee members do not need professional qualifications to represent the views of the public, they are entitled to receive proper training to do their job. This should include an introduction to urban design issues in planning, including the principles set out in this guide and the opportunities to improve design locally through using the planning toolkit.

Member (and officer) training might include seminars on particular themes (such as the design of supermarkets or mixed-use areas).

REVIEWING OUTCOMES

Local authorities need to review the outcome of their contribution to the development process. Regular visits to completed projects will help them reflect on the decisions they took and on the impact made by officers or members in negotiating changes to schemes.

This process will illustrate the successes and failures of development control, and the adequacy of the policies on which it rests. If this experience is properly analysed and understood, it should lead to improved policies and procedures, and to an upward spiral of achieving better design through the planning process.

⬤ THE MARKET SQUARE IN KINGSTON-UPON-HULL FOLLOWING REFURBISHMENT

RAISING STANDARDS IN URBAN DESIGN

PROACTIVE MANAGEMENT

COLLABORATION

DEVELOPING THE RIGHT SKILLS

DESIGN INITIATIVES

MONITORING AND REVIEW

RAISING STANDARDS IN URBAN DESIGN

The effectiveness of the planning tools in raising standards of urban design will depend on how they are used and the management style and ability of the people who use them.

This section is intended to show how local authorities (and others involved in planning and development) can ensure quality, improve the effectiveness of the planning tools, manage the planning process proactively, promote collaborative working, develop design-related skills, and support design initiatives.

Everyone who makes policy, shapes opinions, sets budgets, selects designers, writes briefs or assesses proposals can play a part in raising standards.

PROACTIVE MANAGEMENT

Operating the planning system effectively involves exercising considerable discretion. Plans and supporting documents provide a reference point against which to measure development proposals, not a legally binding yardstick.

At its best, planning manages the process of change proactively, rather than merely reacting to events. The best planning practice involves a real engagement with the process of development. It helps to release development value that might otherwise be locked up in intractable urban problems. Thus it can achieve public policy objectives that might otherwise seem impossible and remove obstacles that might otherwise perpetuate conflict and cause delay.

Achieving this involves the planner in finding out who has a stake in change; bringing together information and opinions from those people; helping to identify common interests; and reaching agreement on planning and design principles. Specific tasks are likely to include: planning, organising and co-ordinating the development briefing process; providing information and communicating; motivating a wide range of people; managing conflict; facilitating events; negotiating; and monitoring and reviewing the process.

The proactive management of the planning and development process is distinctly different from a purely reactive approach. With proactive management:

commercial feasibility is seen as a key to harnessing the development process to achieve the goals of public policy, rather than being regarded as irrelevant to planning. Developers rely on the planning system to reduce uncertainty about the conditions for development, and to help them in complying with public policy objectives, responding to local context, and managing the process of reconciling conflicting interests;

the timing of the planning process is seen as responding to the pace of the development process, rather than proceeding independently of it;

the planning department works closely with other departments and agencies to promote wider corporate objectives, initiatives and socio-economic policy, for example working with the Police on community safety;

there is multi-disciplinary working by all departments of the local authority (including planning, highways and transportation, housing and economic development) and across all disciplines to foster a holistic approach to urban design and development;

development planners and development controllers work closely together in pursuing common objectives. Site development briefs are prepared collaboratively to identify common interests and initiate dialogue in the context of the council's policies, rather than being used merely to set out those policies;

development control is used as a positive means of guiding planning applicants towards fulfilling both their own objectives and those of public policy.

Proactive management requires planning departments to help applicants and potential applicants find their way through the process, particularly by putting them in contact at an early stage with all the council officers with a possible interest in the development. The aim should be to resolve as much as possible of the potential conflict arising from a development proposal. Resolving conflicts early helps to avoid confrontation, polarised attitudes and delay.

⬆ WORKING ACROSS DISCIPLINES TO DELIVER A WELL-DESIGNED TRANSPORT INTERCHANGE IN SUNDERLAND

To do this successfully development control planners should be skilled in negotiation, collaboration and communication. They should be trained in the use of SPG to guide development. It is essential that the council attracts talented planners who are committed to using their skills to make things happen.

COLLABORATION

The outcome of the planning process depends on how effectively people work together: those who guide and control design; those who initiate and implement development; and the designers and those who manage the process.

Do these parties communicate with each other?

Do they negotiate to resolve potential conflicts?

Do the people preparing guidance understand the needs of developers and landowners?

Do the designers work within the constraints of the market?

Do the developers have access to the information they need about the local context?

These connections rarely happen by chance: the creative process by which people collaborate to build on common interests has to be managed. Managing that process is itself a skill. Success depends on using suitable approaches and techniques, holding the right sort of events, and involving the right people, in the right sequence and at the appropriate time.

A local authority or partnership may have the necessary skills itself, or it may need to hire a facilitator or other consultants to plan and support the process of collaboration.

Effective collaboration and public participation can help the urban design process by raising difficult issues at an early stage. Government policy encourages public consultation and participation (in some instances setting out formal requirements) in preparing development plans, SPG, and environmental and conservation area enhancement schemes, and in determining planning applications. Collaboration and public participation are also needed in preparing village design statements, countryside design summaries and regeneration initiatives.

PLANNING FOR REAL HELPS RESIDENTS DETERMINE THEIR OWN PRIORITIES

A DRAWING MAY COMMUNICATE MORE EASILY THAN THE WRITTEN WORD IN A COLLABORATIVE EVENT

The success of collaboration will depend on:

- the process being tailored to local circumstances;

- everyone involved understanding their role, rights and responsibilities from the beginning;

- where appropriate, the process being open to everyone with a stake in the area;

- the flow of information being managed to match the needs of all participants;

- participants having appropriate access to skills and professional expertise.

Successful collaboration involves using appropriate approaches and techniques in a planned and coordinated way, rather than choosing whichever happens to be the favourite of a particular enthusiast. A range of possible approaches and techniques is available, such as:

- design workshops (sometimes known as 'charrettes') bringing a wide range of participants together to explore design ideas for a particular area;

- action planning, community planning weekends and Urban Design Action Teams (UDATs) involving collaboration between local people and an invited team of professionals (often over several days) to explore design ideas for a particular area;

- Planning for Real which enables residents to use a model of their area as a tool to help them determine priorities for the future, with technical experts available 'on tap but not on top';

- Future Search and Open Space, which are techniques for groups of people (as few as five or as many as 800, and over between one and five days) to identify common interests, discuss ideas, share information and experience, and organise themselves into continuing working groups focusing on specific topics.

74

TECHNIQUES

The techniques and equipment used in collaborative events to generate ideas, develop and test options, and take decisions are varied.

- Brainstorming sessions
- Strengths, weaknesses, opportunities and threats (SWOT) or good/bad/ugly analysis
- Key word selection
- Interactive models
- Exhibitions
- Slides
- Overhead projectors
- Videos
- Sketching
- Photomontage

ORGANISING A COLLABORATIVE EVENT

Organisers of collaborative events will need to ask a lengthy series of questions.

- What are the objectives?
- How does the event relate to the continuing processes of planning and design?
- Who are the relevant stakeholders?
- Who hosts the event and sends out the invitations?
- Who will organise the event?
- How long will the event last?
- What sort of venue should be used?
- What equipment or specialised services are needed?
- What will be the cost of the event, preparation and follow-up?

- Who will sponsor the event?
- Who will be invited?
- Who will write the brief or agenda?
- What preparatory work is needed?
- Who will be the facilitator?
- Will an independent facilitator be needed?
- What will be the role of any other professionals?
- Should any limitations be put on participating professionals later accepting related consultancy commissions?
- How will the participants be briefed?
- How will the event be presented to the media?
- What sort of report(s) and/or drawings will be produced?
- How will the event be followed up?
- Who will take responsibility for taking the initiative forward after the event?

A MODEL (THIS ONE IS AT HACKNEY BUILDING EXPLORATORY) CAN PROVIDE AN EFFECTIVE FOCUS FOR DISCUSSION, PARTICULARLY FOR PEOPLE UNUSED TO READING PLANS

RESIDENTS MAKING A SITE VISIT TO COLLECT INFORMATION FOR A COLLABORATIVE DEVELOPMENT BRIEF

Example:

Collaboration in brief-making, Twyford

500 different people, one in ten of the population of Twyford in Berkshire, took part in a project to prepare a development brief for a site of great local importance.

The site

Twyford is a historic village which had no major supermarket. The council, Wokingham District, and traders feared a spiral of decline in shopping facilities. Just behind the main street lay almost two hectares of under-used land. The local plan identified the site for mixed-use development, and promised a development brief, but there was a continuing threat that a developer would bring forward a housing proposal.

An earlier consultation exercise had attempted to establish a vision of the village's future. This persuaded the council to employ an independent facilitator for the public participation, to show that it was not using the exercise merely to engineer support for its own favoured option but to produce a brief supported by the developer, community and local authority.

The council prepared a document defining the objectives and planning requirements for the site, without presenting ideas which might pre-empt consideration of options. This brief, including plans and elevations, was formally adopted by the council, and then widely circulated.

Workshops

The first one-day workshop attracted 100 people. It focused on the area's problems, constraints and opportunities and used elevations and sections of the site at 1:200 scale, cardboard templates of possible developments, familiar buildings in the locality, parking arrangements (from the county design guide) and turning circles for vehicles. The second workshop attracted 200 people. Its purpose was to develop the ideas from the first workshop and explore possible solutions. Participative techniques included a questionnaire on responses to a set of images of places, the selection of 'key words' describing Twyford, and the use of a 1:200 polystyrene model on which blocks of potential buildings could be added or removed. Council officers and the facilitator helped participants express their ideas in the form of sketches.

The council's urban design team then collated the sketch proposals into a series of five options which were displayed at a public exhibition, at which visitors were asked to complete a questionnaire. A final workshop refined the questionnaire responses into a single scheme, again making use of the polystyrene model. The financial feasibility of the various options was assessed using a computer model which the council developed which was accessible by anyone at the workshop. The council's property section also assessed commercial feasibility but the landowners and developers who took part in the workshops declined to do so.

A sense of ownership

The final preferred layout was presented to a public meeting, attended by 180 people, following a leaflet drop to all households in the village. This attracted a number of people who had not noticed any of the widespread publicity in the village and felt aggrieved as a result. Generally these people opposed any development of the site whereas those who had attended the workshops generally supported the recommended proposal.

The outcome

After protracted negotiations, including a planning refusal on design grounds, a supermarket has been built on the site rather than the mixed-used scheme which was envisaged. It is considered locally that although the process was carried out effectively, this result stemmed from the failure of the landowners and developers to be fully committed to the outcome.

DEVELOPING THE RIGHT SKILLS

The extent to which the planning process facilitates good design depends on the skills, knowledge and attitudes of the participants. At present, many of these people lack the full range of skills and depth of knowledge required.

It is especially important that town planners are committed to good design and continue to refresh their skills, particularly those involved in development control. It is not enough for a local authority to have a corporate commitment to high standards of design and access to design expertise from staff urban designers or consultants if those dealing with planning applicants and applications are not interested in design. In these circumstances, even the best design policies, frameworks, guides and briefs are likely to be ineffective.

TARGET GROUPS FOR TRAINING

There is a wide range of people whose attitudes to design helps to determine what will be built. These include:

local authorities – not just planners, urban designers and landscape architects, but elected members who may be unfamiliar with planning and design; administrators and technical staff in planning departments (who all need at least a basic understanding of the council's commitment to design); enforcement officers; highway engineers; and housing managers;

the development sector – among others, developers; surveyors; architects; planning and urban design consultants; estate agents and managers; plan drawers; builders (including volume house-builders); and bankers and financiers. All influence the design process and ultimately the quality of urban design, though many of those involved in drawing up and submitting planning applications may have little or no design training;

those with specific interests – among others, housing association staff; town centre managers; regeneration agencies.

▲ THE LIVERPOOL ARCHITECTURE AND DESIGN TRUST AIMS TO MAKE DESIGN PART OF EVERY ASPECT OF THE CITY'S LIFE.

77

Example:

Sheffield's Heart of the City Project

The centre of Sheffield is being transformed through the 'Heart of the City' project. New public spaces have been created and life brought back to the city centre. Concerns about safety, traffic and the poor quality of paving and planting have been tackled through a multi-disciplinary approach. The illustrated Peace Gardens is now a focus for visitors and residents and has been a spur to private sector investment.

PEACE GARDENS, SHEFFIELD:
THE TRANSFORMATION

PEACE GARDENS, SHEFFIELD: AT NIGHT

78

DESIGN INITIATIVES

A wide range of initiatives has contributed to changing attitudes to design and raising expectations in particular places. These have frequently included a wider range of people than those who are professionally involved in the planning system, including councillors and members of the public.

Initiatives such as the Birmingham Design Initiative and the Kent Design Initiative have promoted high standards of design through competitions, conferences and other projects and have been the product of collaboration between professional practices, higher education, businesses and local authorities.

Urban forums have brought together a wide range of people to consider design issues and collaboration between local authorities has helped to share experience, skills and resources. One example of the latter is the Devon Environment Initiative through which the planning authorities of Devon jointly published a series of guidance notes on important design issues.

Other examples include local or regional design awards (such as Hove Borough Council's annual awards for the best shopfronts); architectural workshops (Newcastle Architectural Workshop combined the roles of community technical aid with environmental education); and information networks (such as the Midlands Know How Network which provided links between a wide range of technical aid services in the region and published a Know How Directory).

⬤ ONE OF A SERIES OF HANDS-ON EXHIBITS
AT HACKNEY BUILDING EXPLORATORY

DESIGN COMPETITIONS

A design competition can help to ensure a high standard of design for the development of an important site, and it can focus public attention on the proposal. The success of a competition depends on having a clear brief, giving competitors realistic expectations of what is on offer, and ensuring that the process is well-conceived. The RIBA can provide advice on holding competitions.

ARCHITECTURE AND PLANNING CENTRES

An architecture and planning centre can become the focus for promoting high standards of design and development. It can provide information; serve as a contact point for networks, skills and professionals; present a city and its region to residents and visitors; present best practice in architecture, urban design and renewal from other places; provide a focal point for communication and collaboration between people and organisations, at all scales from local to citywide.

This requires careful planning and committed backing. There is no reason why the programmes and networks of an architecture and planning centre should not be developed before a building is found or created to house the centre. Centres can draw on existing environmental education and interpretation initiatives, programmes of architectural tours, public consultation and participation programmes, and information services. They can complement the network of existing support services such as planning aid and community technical aid, which provide access to advice and skills for people and organisations which might otherwise have to do without. Examples of such centres include the Architecture Foundation, the Kent Architecture Centre and the Liverpool Architecture and Design Trust.

80

Example:

A quality audit, Westminster

An extract from Westminster City Council's publication reporting on the planning department's audit of its work:

The Development Division is undertaking a continuing Quality Audit of its activities. The audit has been devised to assess the handling of a significant number of typical development proposals to ensure that the outcomes comply with relevant policy and have indeed been enhanced by the intervention of officers through their negotiations and recommendations.

The proposals illustrated range from simple alterations and extensions to major developments; from Town Scheme grants to the provision of disabled access; and from enforcement to environmental improvements. Quality can be added to a scheme by the removal of bulk to safeguard residential amenity; by the addition of residential units to an all-office scheme; by the reinstatement of historic townscape; by the retention of a tree; by encouraging the highest standards of new design; or by the restoration of original features.

Most of these schemes have been carefully negotiated and ultimately granted permission. However, others were considered to be so unacceptable that they were refused. These refusals are in themselves qualitative acts, as a refusal is a clear indication of an intention to accept nothing other than high standards.

MONITORING AND REVIEW

Design policy in development plans and supplementary planning guidance should be monitored to check how it is being used, and how developers and planning applicants are responding to it. As a result the guidance itself may need to be reviewed, or it may be necessary to review its promotion, marketing and the associated training.

The impact of policy and guidance should be assessed by looking at completed buildings and schemes, and the results of appeals, not just at the quality of planning applications. This can involve members of the planning committee, as well as council officers.

Meetings with local architects, designers, developers, Police and interest groups can help to establish how guidance is being received. Parish councils, civic and amenity societies, and conservation and design advisory panels may help in this process. The impact of design policy and guidance may also be monitored through a local authority's quality audit and awards schemes.

△ AWARDS HELP TO RAISE AWARENESS OF DESIGN

QUALITY AUDITS

The impact of design policy and guidance needs to be constantly monitored so that they can be reviewed and revised as necessary. Local authorities conduct audits of their management of the design and planning process in order to:

- satisfy Best Value and Citizen's Charter objectives;

- assess the impact of the council's actions at every stage in the planning process;

- ensure that the council's design policies are being applied effectively and that SPG is being followed;

- contribute to the review of design policy and guidance;

- learn from planning appeal decisions.

Quality audits can be carried out either by the council's own officers, by another local authority or agency, or by consultants. A quality audit checklist might set out the following details relating to a particular planning application:

- the main issues raised by the development proposal;

- the mechanisms used in guiding and processing the development proposal, and how (and with what success) they were applied;

- the relevant policies in the development plan, and whether the development complied with them when built.

Such an audit can also be an effective way of communicating the council's commitment to design and explaining the planning process to non-specialists.

Other methods of assessing the impact of design policy and guidance include:

- visits by council members and officers and others to completed buildings and schemes;

- internal workshops;

- comments by a design advisory panel;

- design awards;

- views expressed by estate agents on commercial viability and rates of lettings;

- views expressed by residents' groups and amenity societies on the impact of new development.

APPENDICES

Checklists

Glossary

Further reading

Some useful contacts

Acknowledgements

Image credits

CHECKLIST 1

Is design working for you?

This checklist can be used by local planning authorities as the basis for selecting priorities.

Design policies (page 44)
- Does the development plan contain design policies?

- Do the policies include general, area-specific and topic-based design policies?

- Are the design policies expressed at the right level of specificity?

Supplementary planning guidance (page 46)
- Is the development plan supported by supplementary planning guidance:

  – urban design frameworks?

  – development briefs?

  – design guides?

- Does the council need internal guidance notes on preparing supplementary planning guidance?

Urban design frameworks (page 48)
- Does the council need urban design frameworks as a means of creating confidence, unlocking potential, managing change, providing a strategy for implementation, and expressing design and planning concepts and proposals in two- and three-dimensions?

Development briefs (page 53)
- Does the council produce development briefs as a means of implementing its design and planning policies?

- Does the council produce development briefs jointly with other organisations, where appropriate?

- Does the council set out its expectations for any development briefs it does not prepare itself, and the procedure for preparing them?

- Does the council have sufficient design expertise to manage consultants effectively or to assess the design element of a developer's brief, in cases where the council itself does not prepare a development brief?

Design guides (page 57)
- Does the council need a more comprehensive series of design guides?

- Are design guides prepared in collaboration with all relevant departments of the local authority (and other local authorities if appropriate) and with other relevant organisations?

- Are the public and potential users consulted effectively when design guides are being prepared?

- Are design guides sent out with planning application forms?

- Do design guides have the status of supplementary planning guidance?

- Does the council hold internal seminars with elected members and officers to share experience and ensure commitment to implement the guides?

- Does the council hold seminars with potential users of its design guides?

- Are design guides promoted through other publications and visits to show how they can lead to higher standards of design?

- Do staff have the necessary negotiation skills to ensure that development complies with the principles of the design guide?

Design statements (page 66)

- Does the council insist on design statements being submitted with planning applications, to help in evaluating development proposals against its own design policies and Government guidance?

- Does the council use design statements to structure the design and planning process in relation to sites which are not the subject of development briefs?

Design assessments (page 67)

- Does the council commission independent assessments of development proposals, where it does not have adequate design skills itself (in view of the scale or sensitivity of the proposed development)?

Collaboration (page 73)

- Is the council making the most of collaboration and public participation as a means of resolving conflicts early in the design and development process and avoiding unnecessary confrontation, polarised attitudes and delay?

Skills (page 77)

- Does the Council employ staff with appropriate design skills?

- Does the council have a training and education programme to ensure that everyone involved in design and planning has the necessary skills and knowledge of design appropriate to their role?

Design initiatives (page 79)

- Is the council active in promoting awareness of design, highlighting good practice and facilitating joint working through design initiatives?

Quality audits (page 81)

- Does the council conduct quality audits to assess how it is managing the design and planning process, and the effectiveness of its design policies and guidance?

CHECKLIST 2

INFORMATION REQUIREMENTS FOR A PLANNING APPLICATION

Adequate plans and drawings must be submitted as part of a planning application, so that the design can be properly assessed. They will be required for the benefit of planners, councillors (on planning and other committees), residents and amenity groups, among others. The checklist sets out what is likely to be required for full (as opposed to outline) applications. Models and computer-based representations are particularly useful in the case of large scale or complex development proposals.

Location plan
- Scale 1:1250 preferably, and no smaller than 1:2500. Metric scales only.
- North point, date and number.
- Outline the application property, and indicate any adjoining property owned or controlled by the applicant.
- Show the application property in relation to all adjoining properties and the immediate surrounding area, including roads.
- Show vehicular access to a highway if the site does not adjoin a highway.

Details of existing site layout
- Scale, typically 1:200.
- North point, date and number on plans.
- Show the whole property, including all buildings, gardens, open spaces and car parking.
- Tree survey, where appropriate.

Details of proposed site layout
- Scale, typically 1:200.
- North point, date and number on plans.
- Show the siting of any new building or extension, vehicular/pedestrian access, changes in levels, landscape proposals, including trees to be removed, new planting, new or altered boundary walls and fences, and new hard-surfaced open spaces.
- Show proposals in the context of adjacent buildings.

Floor plans
- Scale 1:50 or 1:100.
- In the case of an extension, show the floor layout of the existing building to indicate the relationship between the two, clearly indicating what is new work.
- Show floor plans in the context of adjacent buildings, where appropriate.
- In the case of minor applications it may be appropriate to combine the layout and floor plan (unless any demolition is involved).
- Include a roof plan where necessary to show a complex roof or alterations to one.

Elevations
- Scale 1:50 or 1:100 (consistent with floor plans).
- Show every elevation of a new building or extension.
- For an extension or alteration, clearly distinguish existing and proposed elevations.
- Include details of materials and external appearance.
- Show elevations in the context of adjacent buildings, where appropriate.

Cross sections

- Scale 1:50 or 1:100 (consistent with floor plans).

- Provide these if appropriate.

Design statement

Design statements submitted with planning applications should:

- Explain the design principles and design concept.

- Explain how the design relates to its wider context (through a full context appraisal where appropriate).

The written design statement should be illustrated, as appropriate, by:

- Plans and elevations.

- Photographs of the site and its surroundings.

- Other illustrations, such as perspectives.

Other supporting material

- For example, retail, environmental or transport assessments.

GLOSSARY

This glossary is intended to provide general guidance, not authoritative definitions of terms which are sometimes controversial or used with different meanings in different contexts.

Accessibility The ability of people to move round an area and to reach places and facilities, including elderly and disabled people, those with young children and those encumbered with luggage or shopping.

Action planning Participation techniques, including community planning weekends and Urban Design Action Teams (UDATs), which enable local people and invited teams of professionals to explore design ideas for particular areas over one or several days.

Activity spine Street or streets along which activity is concentrated.

Activity node Concentration of activity at a particular point.

Adaptability The capacity of a building or space to be changed so as to respond to changing social, technological and economic conditions.

Area appraisal An assessment of an area's land uses, built and natural environment, and social and physical characteristics.

Architecture and planning centre An institution which provides a focus for a range of activities and services (such as discussions, information, exhibitions, collaboration and professional services) relating to architecture and planning.

Brief This guide refers to site-specific briefs as development briefs. Site-specific briefs are also called a variety of other names, including design briefs, planning briefs and development frameworks.

Building elements Doors, windows, cornices and other features which contribute to the overall design of a building.

Building envelope guidelines Diagram(s) with dimensions showing the possible site and massing of a building.

Building exploratory A centre for explaining, interpreting and providing information on the built environment.

Building line The line formed by the frontages of buildings along a street. The building line can be shown on a plan or section.

Bulk The combined effect of the arrangement, volume and shape of a building or group of buildings. Also called massing.

Character assessment An area appraisal identifying distinguishing physical features and emphasising historical and cultural associations.

Charrette An event (ranging from a couple of hours to several days) which brings together a range of people to discuss design issues. A charrette may or may not use techniques of collaborative design. Also known as a design workshop.

Conservation area character appraisal A published document defining the special architectural or historic interest which warranted the area being designated.

Context The setting of a site or area, including factors such as traffic, activities and land uses as well as landscape and built form.

Context (or site and area) appraisal A detailed analysis of the features of a site or area (including land uses, built and natural environment, and social and physical characteristics) which serves as the basis for an urban design framework, development brief, design guide or other policy or guidance.

Countryside design summary Supplementary planning guidance prepared by a local authority to encourage a more regionally and locally based approach to design and planning.

Crime Pattern Analysis Carried out by the Police and is available through liaison with the Architectural Liaison Officer/Crime Prevention Design Adviser. It comprises four components: crime series identification, trend identification, 'hot-spot' analysis and general profile analysis. This last aspect includes an examination of demographic and social change and its impact on criminality and law enforcement.

Defensible space Public and semi-public space that is 'defensible' in the sense that it is surveyed, demarcated or maintained by somebody. Derived from Oscar Newman's 1973 study of the same name, and an important concept in securing public safety in urban areas, defensible space is also dependent upon the existence of escape routes and the level of anonymity which can be anticipated by the users of the space.

Density The floorspace of a building or buildings or some other unit measure in relation to a given area of land. Built density can be expressed in terms of plot ratio (for commercial development); number of units or habitable rooms per hectare (for residential development); site coverage plus the number of floors or a maximum building height; or a combination of these.

Design advisory panel A group of people (often architects) with specialist knowledge, which advises a local authority on the design merits of planning applications or other design issues. Also known as an architects panel.

Design assessment An independent assessment of a design usually carried out for a local authority by consultants, another local authority or some other agency.

Design guide A document providing guidance on how development can be carried out in accordance with the design policies of a local authority or other organisation often with a view to retaining local distinctiveness.

Design principle An expression of one of the basic design ideas at the heart of an urban design framework, design guide, development brief or a development.

Design standards Specific, usually quantifiable measures of amenity and safety in residential areas.

Design statement (a) A pre-application design statement is made by a developer to indicate the design principles on which a development proposal in progress is based. It enables the local authority to give an initial response to the main issues raised by the proposal. (b) A planning application design statement sets out the design principles that the planning applicant has adopted in relation to the site and its wider context, as required by PPG1.

Design workshop see 'charrette'.

Desire line An imaginary line linking facilities or places which people would find it convenient to travel between easily.

89

Development brief A document, prepared by a local planning authority, a developer, or jointly, providing guidance on how a site of significant size or sensitivity should be developed. Site-specific briefs are sometimes known as planning briefs, design briefs and development frameworks.

Development form See 'form'.

Elevation The facade of a building, or the drawing of a facade.

Enclosure The use of buildings to create a sense of defined space.

Energy efficiency The extent to which the use of energy is reduced through the way in which buildings are constructed and arranged on site.

Feasibility The viability of development in relation to economic and market conditions.

Fenestration The arrangement of windows on a facade.

Figure and ground (or figure/ground, or Nolli) diagram A plan showing the relationship between built form and publicly accessible space (including streets) by presenting the former in black and the latter as a white background (or the other way round).

Form The layout (structure and urban grain), density, scale (height and massing), appearance (materials and details) and landscape of development.

Fruin analysis A method of analysing pedestrian movement devised by Bernard Fruin. It applies a 'level of service' concept to pedestrian flows. Fruin defined capacity and speeds of movement in various forms of corridors, pavements and other pedestrian routes.

Future Search A participation technique enabling groups of people to identify common interests, discuss ideas and share information and experience. 'Open space' is a similar technique.

Grain See 'urban grain'.

Height The height of a building can be expressed in terms of a maximum number of floors; a maximum height of parapet or ridge; a maximum overall height; any of these maximum heights in combination with a maximum number of floors; a ratio of building height to street or space width; height relative to particular landmarks or background buildings; or strategic views.

Human scale The use within development of elements which relate well in size to an individual human being and their assembly in a way which makes people feel comfortable rather than overwhelmed.

In-curtilage parking Parking within a building's site boundary, rather than on a public street or space.

Independent design audit An assessment of a design, carried out for a local authority by consultants, another local authority or some other agency.

Indicative sketch A drawing of building forms and spaces which is intended to convey the basic elements of a possible design.

Landmark A building or structure that stands out from its background by virtue of height, size or some other aspect of design.

Landscape The character and appearance of land, including its shape, form, ecology, natural features, colours and elements and the way these components combine. Landscape character can be expressed through landscape appraisal, and maps or plans. In towns 'townscape' describes the same concept.

Layout The way buildings, routes and open spaces are placed in relation to each other.

Layout structure The framework or hierarchy of routes that connect in the local area and at wider scales.

Legibility The degree to which a place can be easily understood and traversed.

Live edge Provided by a building or other feature whose use is directly accessible from the street or space which it faces; the opposite effect to a blank wall.

Local distinctiveness The positive features of a place and its communities which contribute to its special character and sense of place.

Lynchian analysis The widely used method of context appraisal devised by the urban designer Kevin Lynch. It focuses on gateways to an area, nodes, landmarks, views and vistas, and edges and barriers.

Massing The combined effect of the height, bulk and silhouette of a building or group of buildings.

Mixed uses A mix of uses within a building, on a site or within a particular area. 'Horizontal' mixed uses are side by side, usually in different buildings. 'Vertical' mixed uses are on different floors of the same building.

Modal split How the total number of journeys in an area or to a destination is split between different means of transport, such as train, bus, car, walking and cycling.

Movement People and vehicles going to and passing through buildings, places and spaces. The movement network can be shown on plans, by space syntax analysis, by highway designations, by figure and ground diagrams, through data on origins and destinations or pedestrian flows, by desire lines, by details of public transport services, by walk bands or by details of cycle routes.

Natural surveillance (or supervision) The discouragement to wrong-doing by the presence of passers-by or the ability of people to be seen out of surrounding windows. Also known as passive surveillance (or supervision).

Node A place where activity and routes are concentrated often used as a synonym for junction.

Passive surveillance See 'natural surveillance'.

Performance criterion (pl. criteria) A means of assessing the extent to which a development achieves a particular functional requirement (such as maintaining privacy). This contrasts with a standard, which specifies how a development is to be designed (by setting out minimum distances between buildings, for example). The art of urban design lies in balancing principles which may conflict. Standards may be too inflexible to be of use in achieving a balance. Performance criteria, on the other hand, make no prior assumptions about the means of achieving a balance.

Permeability The degree to which an area has a variety of pleasant, convenient and safe routes through it.

Perspective Illustration showing the view from a particular point as it would be seen by the human eye.

Placecheck A type of urban design audit advocated by the Urban Design Alliance, based on the Connected City approach. A local collaborative alliance or partnership uses checklists to investigate the connections in the built environment, in its movement network and among the people who shape it. The Placecheck becomes the first step in a continuing collaborative process of urban design.

Planning brief This guide refers to site-specific briefs as development briefs. Other names, including planning briefs, design briefs and development frameworks are also used.

Planning for Real A participation technique (pioneered by the Neighbourhood Initiatives Foundation) that involves residents and others with an interest coming together to make a model of their area and using it to help them determine their priorities for the future.

Planning Policy Guidance notes (PPGs) Documents embodying Government guidance on general and specific aspects of planning policy to be taken into account in formulating development plan policies and in making planning decisions.

Plot ratio A measurement of density generally expressed as gross floor area divided by the net site area.

Proactive development control Any process by which a local authority works with potential planning applicants to improve the quality of development proposals as early as possible before a planning application is submitted.

Public art Permanent or temporary physical works of art visible to the general public, whether part of the building or free-standing: can include sculpture, lighting effects, street furniture, paving, railings and signs.

Public domain The parts of a village, town or city (whether publicly or privately owned) that are available, without charge, for everyone to use or see, including streets, squares and parks. Also called public realm.

Public/private interface The point at which public areas and buildings meet private ones.

Public realm See 'public domain'

Quality audit A review of its management of the design and planning process by a local authority or other organisation.

Scale The impression of a building when seen in relation to its surroundings, or the size of parts of a building or its details, particularly as experienced in relation to the size of a person. Sometimes it is the total dimensions of a building which give it its sense of scale: at other times it is the size of the elements and the way they are combined. The concept is a difficult and ambiguous one: often the word is used simply as a synonym for 'size'. See 'Human scale'.

Section Drawing showing a slice through a building or site.

Settlement pattern The distinctive way that the roads, paths and buildings are laid out in a particular place.

Sight line The line of sight from a travelling vehicle or person. Sight lines will help to determine how fast vehicles are likely to move and how safe other road users are likely to be.

Space syntax analysis A technique for analysing movement through urban space and predicting the amount of activity likely to result from that movement.

Spine Street or streets along which activity is concentrated.

Strategic view The line of sight from a particular point to an important landmark or skyline.

Street furniture Structures in and adjacent to the highway which contribute to the street scene, such as bus shelters, litter bins, seating, lighting, railings and signs.

Success factor One of the characteristics of a place (or places in general) that tends to make it attractive to live in, work in, or visit. Success factors can be expressed as design principles.

Surveillance The discouragement to wrong-doing by the presence of passers-by or the ability of people to be seen from surrounding windows.

Sustainable development Defined by the Brundtland Commission (1987, and quoted in PPG1) as 'Development which meets present needs without compromising the ability of future generations to achieve their own needs and aspirations'. The UK's strategy for sustainable development "A better quality of life" was published in May 1999 and highlights the need for environmental improvement, social justice and economic success to go hand-in-hand.

Tissue study Comparison of scale and layout of different settlements. This technique makes use of overprinting or tracing maps of successful places over the proposed development site or area, at the same scale. Its gives the designer a clue to the capacity of a place and how it may be structured.

Topography A description or representation of artificial or natural features on or of the ground.

Urban design The art of making places. Urban design involves the design of buildings, groups of buildings, spaces and landscapes, in villages, towns and cities, and the establishment of frameworks and processes which facilitate successful development.

Urban design framework A document which informs the preparation of development plan policies, or sets out in detail how they are to be implemented in a particular area where there is a need to control, guide and promote change. Area development frameworks are also called a variety of other names, including urban design strategies, area development frameworks, spatial masterplans, and planning and urban design frameworks.

Urban grain The pattern of the arrangement and size of buildings and their plots in a settlement; and the degree to which an area's pattern of street-blocks and street junctions is respectively small and frequent, or large and infrequent.

Vernacular The way in which ordinary buildings were built in a particular place, making use of local styles, techniques and materials and responding to local economic and social conditions.

View What is visible from a particular point. Compare 'Vista'.

Vista An enclosed view, usually a long and narrow one.

Visual clutter The uncoordinated arrangement of street furniture, signs and other features.

Village appraisal A study identifying a local community's needs and priorities.

Village design statement An advisory document, usually produced by a village community, suggesting how development might be carried out in harmony with the village and its setting. A village design statement can be given weight by being approved as supplementary planning guidance. The use of village design statements is promoted by the Countryside Agency.

Walk band A line on a map or plan showing the furthest distance that can be walked from a particular point at an average pace in a certain time (usually five or ten minutes).

93

FURTHER READING

Aldous, T. (1992) *Urban Villages*, London, Urban Villages Group.

Alexander, C. et al, (1987) *A New Theory of Urban Design*, New York, Oxford University.

Association of Chief Police Officers et al, (1999) *The Secured by Design Award Scheme*.

Barton, B. Davis, G. Guise, R., (1995) *Sustainable Settlements: a guide for planners, designers and developers*, University of the West of England and Local Government Management Board.

Bentley, I. et al (1985) *Responsive Environments: a manual for designers*, London, Architectural Press.

Broadbent, G. (1990) *Emerging Concepts in Urban Design*, New York, Van Nostrand Reinhold.

Civic Trust and English Historic Towns Forum (1993) *Traffic Measures in Historic Towns*.

Clifford, S. and King, A. (1993) *Local Distinctiveness: place, particularity and identity*, London, Common Ground.

Countryside Commission and English Nature (1996) *The character of England: landscape, wildlife and natural features*.

Coupland, A. (1997) *Reclaiming the City: mixed-use development*, London, Chapman & Hall.

Cowan, R. (1997) *The Connected City*, London, Urban Initiatives.

Davis, C. J., Royal Fine Art Commission (1997) *Improving Design in the High Street*, London, Architectural Press.

Department of the Environment (1994) *Vital and Viable Town Centres: meeting the challenge*, HMSO.

Department of the Environment and Department of Transport (1995) *PPG13: a guide to better practice*, HMSO.

DETR (1998) *Places, Streets and Movement: a companion guide to Design Bulletin 32*.

DETR (1998) *Planning and Development Briefs: a guide to better practice*.

DETR (1998) *Planning for Sustainable Development: towards better practice*.

Duany, A. and Plater-Zyberk, E. (1991) *Towns and Town-Making Principles*, New York, Rizzoli International Publications.

English Heritage (1997) Conservation Area Appraisals.

English Partnerships and the Housing Corporation (2000) *Urban Design Compendium*.

Gehl, J. (1996) *Life Between Buildings: Using Public Space*, Copenhagen, Arkitektens Forlag.

Greed, C. and Roberts, M. (eds.) (1998) *Introducing Urban Design: interventions and responses*, Harlow, Longman.

Hall, A. C. (1996) *Design Control: towards a new approach*, Oxford, Butterworth Architecture.

Hillier, B. (1996) *Space is the Machine: a configurational theory of architecture*, Cambridge, Cambridge University Press.

Jacobs, A. (1993) *Great Streets*, Massachusetts, MIT Press.

Hayward, R. and McGlynn, S. (eds.) (1993) *Making Better Places: urban design now*, Oxford, Joint Centre for Urban Design.

Katz, P. (1994) *The New Urbanism: towards an architecture of community*, New York, McGraw-Hill.

Kostof, Spiro (1991) *The City Shaped: urban patterns and meaning throughout history*, London, Bullfinch.

Kostof, Spiro (1992) *The City Assembled: the elements of urban form through history*, Boston, Bullfinch.

Landry, C. and Bianchini, F. (1995) *The Creative City*, London, Demos in association with Comedia.

Littlefair, P. J. (1991) *Site Layout Planning for Daylight and Sunlight: a guide to good practice*, London, Building Research Establishment Report.

Lynch, K. (1984) *Good City Form*, Massachusetts, MIT Press.

Lynch, K. (1990) *The Image of the City*, Massachusetts, MIT Press.

Moughtin, C. (1992) *Urban Design: street and square*, Oxford, Butterworth Architecture.

Punter, J. and Carmona, M. (1997) *The Design Dimension of Planning: theory, content and best practice for design policies*, London, E & FN Spon.

Sennett, R. (1990) *The Conscience of the Eye: the design and social life of cities*, London, Faber & Faber.

The Prince's Foundation (2000) *Planning by Design not Default*.

Tibbalds, F. (1992) *Making People-Friendly Towns: improving the public environment in towns and cities*, London, Longman Press.

Tugnutt, A. Robertson, M. (1987) *Making Townscape: a contextual approach to building in an urban setting*, London, Mitchell Publishing.

Urban Task Force (1999) *Towards an Urban Renaissance*, DETR.

Wates, N. (1996) *Action Planning*, London, Prince of Wales's Institute of Architecture.

Wates, N. (2000) *The Community Planning Handbook*, Earthscan.

Worpole, K., Greenhalgh, L. (1996) *The Freedom of the City*, London, Demos.

SOME USEFUL CONTACTS

ARCHITECTURE CENTRES (FORMING THE ARCHITECTURE CENTRE NETWORK):

CUBE
117 Portland Street
Manchester M1 6FB
Tel: 0161 237 5525
Fax: 0161 236 5815

Hackney Building Exploratory
The Professional Development Centre
Albion Drive
London EB 4ET
Tel/Fax: 020 7275 8555

Liverpool Architecture and Design Trust
16 Vernon Street
Liverpool L2
Tel: 0151 233 4079
Fax: 0151 233 4078

Northern Architecture
Blackfriars
Newcastle-upon-Tyne NE1 4XN
Tel/Fax: 0191 260 2191

Kent Architecture Centre
Chatham Historic Dockyard
Chatham ME4 4TE
Tel: 01634 401166
Fax: 01634 403302

RIBA Architecture Gallery
Portland Place
London SW1P 3NQ
Tel: 020 7307 3699
Fax: 020 7307 3703

RIBA Eastern Region Architecture Centre
Lumley Architects
37 Tunwells Lane
Cambridge CB2 5LJ
Tel: 01223 509 183
Fax: 01223 509 185

The Architecture Centre
Narrow Quay
Bristol BS1 4QA
Tel: 0117 922 1540
Fax: 0117 922 1541

Association of Chief Police Officers Crime Prevention Initiatives
Deputy Company Secretery
25 Victoria Street
London SW1H 0EX
Tel: 020 7227 3434
Fax: 020 7227 3400
www.securedbydesign.com

Building Research Establishment
Tel: 01923 664 000
Email: enquiries@bre.co.uk

Civic Trust
17 Carlton House Terrace
London SW1Y 5AW
Tel: 020 7930 0914
Fax: 020 7321 0180

Countryside Agency
John Dower House
Crescent Place
Cheltenham
Gloucestershire GL50 3RA
Tel: 01242 521 381
Fax: 01242 584 270

96

English Heritage
Customer Services
PO Box 9019
London WIA OJA
Tel: 020 7973 3434

English Historic Towns Forum
PO Box 22
Frenchay
Bristol BS16 1RZ
Tel: 0117 975 0459
Fax: 0117 975 0460

English Nature
Northminster House
Peterborough PE1 1UA
Tel: 01733 455 000
Fax: 01733 568 834
Email: enquiries@english-nature.org.uk

Institution of Civil Engineers
1 Great George Street
Westminster
London SWIP 3AA
Tel: 020 7222 7722
Fax: 020 7222 7500

Landscape Institute
6-8 Barnard Mews
London WIN 4AD
Tel: 020 7738 9166
Fax: 020 7738 9134
Email: mail@l-i.org.uk

Local Government Association
Local Government House
Smith Square
London SWIP 3HZ
Tel: 020 7664 3000
Fax: 020 7664 3030
Email: info@lga.gov.uk

National Disability Council
Level 4A
Caxton House
Tothill Street
London SWIH 9NA
Tel: 0207 273 5636
Fax: 0207 273 5929

Royal Institute of British Architects
66 Portland Place
London WIN 4AD
Tel: 020 7307 3677
Fax: 020 7230 2379

Royal Institution of Chartered Surveyors
12 Great George Street
Parliament Square
London SWIP 3AD
Tel: 020 7334 3751
Fax: 020 7334 3795
Email: info@rics.org.uk

Royal Town Planning Institute
26 Portland Place
London WIN 4BE
Tel: 020 7636 9107
Fax: 020 7323 1582
Email: online@rtpi.org.uk

Urban Design Group
6 Ashbrook Courtyard
Westbrook Street
Blewbury
Oxon OX11 9QA
Tel: 01235 851 415
Fax: 01235 851 410
Email: admin@udg.org.uk

Urban Villages Forum
70-77 Cowcross Street
London
EC1M 6BP

97

ACKNOWLEDGEMENTS

This guide is based on work by a team of consultants led by Kelvin Campbell of Urban Initiatives and Robert Cowan. The project team was drawn from Urban Initiatives and specialist advice was provided by Paul Murrain, John Punter, Jim Redwood, Les Sparks and Kim Wilkie.

The published guide has been prepared by the Department of the Environment, Transport and the Regions in partnership with the Commission for Architecture and the Built Environment.

The Department, Commission and consultants wish to thank all those who contributed to the development of this guide, including the assistance provided by members of the project's sounding board and the Urban Design Alliance.

IMAGE CREDITS

Barton Willmore Partnership, p54 (right)

Bill Hopper Design Ltd, p68

Birmingham City Council, p20, 21, 52 (top)

BrindleyPlace Plc, p27 (left), 32 (bottom left)

Bristol City Council, p17, 43

Bristol City Council Planning Department, *Bristol City Centre Draft Local Plan*, p48 (bottom)

Corporation of London, p45 (bottom)

Countryside Agency, front cover (bottom left), p19 (top)

Crown Regeneration, Glasgow, p12, 33

Duchy of Cornwall, p23

ECD Architects, p24

EDAW, p50

Image Visual Communications, p73

Kingston-upon-Hull City Council, p48 (example), 69

Leicester City Council, p64

Manhattan Loft Corporation, p31 (top left)

Mendip District Council, p52 (bottom)

Moss Side and Hulme Partnership, p63

Profile Photo Agency, p34, 69

RIBA, p29 (bottom right), 30 (top) 31 (bottom left)

Robert Cowan, p75 (both images), 77, 79

Roger Evans Associates, p49

Sheffield Design and Property, p4, 26, 29 (top), 78 (example), 82

Space Syntax Laboratory, p38

Urban Task Force, *Towards an Urban Renaissance*, p9

Westminster City Council, p80 (example)

All other images have been provided by Urban Initiatives.